CW00957446

Radioactive I
For Radio, Sta

Marina Caldarone has trained actors at most of Britain's
leading drama schools. She has been a theatre director since
1984, twelve years of which as Associate Director of Theatr
Clwyd and Artistic Director of the Queen's Theatre,
Hornchurch, and is a freelance radio drama producer. She is
also an acting coach in television, regular lecturer on
contemporary theatre, and has co-written *Actions, An Actors
Thesaurus*, with Maggie Lloyd Williams. She is Drama
Director of Crying Out Loud, a production company making
voice-over CDs for actors.

Marilyn Le Conte is lecturer in radio acting at the Royal
Welsh College of Music and Drama, and teaches radio
modules at the Liverpool Institute for Performing Arts. A
Drama and French graduate of Hull University, she also
continues to work as an actress, and as a dialect consultant in
radio, television, film, theatre, opera, business and
education. She lives near Cardiff with her husband and two
sons.

Radio*active* Duologues
For Radio, Stage and Screen

Edited by

MARINA CALDARONE

and

MARILYN LE CONTE

Methuen Drama

Published by Methuen Drama

10 9 8 7 6 5 4 3 2 1

Copyright in this selection and editors' notes © Marina Caldarone and
Marilyn Le Conte, 2006
The editors have asserted their moral rights
Copyright in the foreword © 2006 by Gordon House

A CIP catalogue record for this book is available from the British Library

ISBN 978 0 413 77578 8

Available in the USA from Bloomsbury Academic & Professional,
175 Fifth Avenue/3rd Floor, New York, NY 10010.
www.BloomsburyAcademicUSA.com

Typeset by SX Composing DTP, Rayleigh, Essex

Printed and bound in Great Britain by

CPI Antony Rowe, Chippenham and Eastbourne

Disclaimer
Methuen Drama gratefully acknowledges the permissions granted
to reproduce the quoted extracts within this work. Every effort has been made to
trace the current copyright holders of the extracts included in this work. The
publishers apologise for any unintended omissions and would be pleased to
receive any information that would enable them to amend any inaccuracies or
omissions in future editions.

Contents

Foreword

How satisfying to be asked to write a foreword for a book that focuses primarily on audition pieces for radio. As someone who has directed well over three hundred plays for this wonderful but hugely undervalued medium, I have done my fair share of auditioning, and I have not been the first director to groan inwardly (and occasionally outwardly) as another enthusiastic young actor prepares to give me his or her fresh interpretation of a stage-play monologue that I've heard so often I could almost quote it by heart. ('If I have to listen to one more rendition of Ophelia losing it, I shall go mad myself,' as one colleague memorably put it.)

The great virtue of this book is that the two writers – themselves long-term radio enthusiasts – have chosen extracts not merely from contemporary stage writing, but from recent radio plays as well. Alongside the likes of Alan Ayckbourn, Shelagh Stephenson and Martin Crimp (who have nonetheless written for radio themselves) there are writers who are perhaps less well known to a theatregoing audience. Yet today's radio drama would be much the weaker without contributions from such masters of the medium as Michael Butt, Sheila Goff, Katie Hims or Sebastian Baczkiewicz. Listen to an original play or a dramatisation (such as *The Pallisers*) by Martyn Wade and you know immediately that the writing – dare I say it – will be of a higher quality than much of what you find on television or on the stage. That is not to say that all radio drama is of a universally high standard; with so many play slots to fill, and with minimum recording time for all but the most expensive projects, it is inevitable that some plays fail to engage. But the best radio writing – and the best radio acting – compares very favourably with work produced for any of the more glamorous visual media.

The extracts in this book can, of course, be used as audition pieces for stage, television or film, but some of the radio-play extracts give clues as to what makes this medium distinctive. Take Katie Hims's

Man with a Travel Hairdryer: here, Dean, in his revealing and often very funny voice-overs, speaks directly to the radio audience, letting us share completely his inner life, his secret thoughts. Now, a voice-over can be used in any medium, but only on radio does it have real intimacy and intensity. Act this scene on the stage and however *sotto voce* the director makes Dean's 'thoughts', the lines still have to be projected sufficiently to reach the paying customer at the back of the stalls. On radio we're in Dean's head; there's no need to project a single line of his confessional; he talks directly to us, and each scene is the stronger for this direct contact between character and listener.

In *The Employee*, Sebastian Baczkiewicz takes radio's unique strength – allowing us to see the inner lives of characters – one stage further. Rather than the voice-over, he enables one character's fantasies – Adam's – to be revealed in the dialogue of those to whom he is talking. Thus while he argues with his ex-wife outside a Japanese restaurant, his wife suddenly starts to speak Japanese – a language with which she is totally unfamiliar. This is, of course, impossible; but in a medium where words are all-important it beautifully demonstrates how Adam is losing his grip on reality.

Radio flits more easily than any other medium between reality and fantasy. A few carefully selected CDs and proper signposting by the writer and you can be exploring Mars or trapped inside a gigantic Mars bar. Indeed, inanimate objects may have a radio life of their own. In Sheila Goff's *File it Under Fiction*, there is a scene preceding the one included in this selection that appears totally naturalistic: Simon explains to Ann in a large bookshop that he is awaiting the arrival of a blind date, and that they will recognise each other when she says that she is 'seeking Madame Bovary'. However, as soon as he picks up the requisite book, and opens it at a random page, we hear the sound of a horse-drawn carriage and passionate lovemaking. '*Rowdy buggers, books. They're at it all the time, clattering away between the covers . . .*' says Simon, nonchalantly, shutting the book, and magically switching off the sound effect. And we, the radio audience, quite nonchalantly accept this device.

On radio, words and sound effects are what drive the narrative along.

There are those who say that radio drama's great days are long gone; that wonderful radio plays are now rarely written and that the medium that first nurtured Pinter and Orton, Stoppard and Beckett no longer makes the same startling dramatic discoveries that it once did. To which I would reply that the discovery of new talent is at the very heart of what radio drama does. Lee Hall, Anthony Minghella and Debbie Green are more recent names to add to the Pinter/Beckett pantheon, while there are writers in this book – David Eldridge, Tanika Gupta, Howard Barker among others – who regularly write for radio alongside other media.

And as for radio drama being impoverished, just look at the huge variety of drama slots available on network radio in any week. They range from Radio 3's Sunday play (generally ninety minutes or more) to the fifteen-minute *Woman's Hour* serial; there's a play on Radio 4 every afternoon, the *Classic Serial* on Sunday, challenging contemporary plays on a Friday evening, the series of innovative, personal radio dramas in Radio 3's *The Wire*, an hour-long play on BBC World Service every weekend – and I haven't even mentioned *The Archers* or the Asian Network's soap *Silver Street*. This isn't a medium that's dying; far from it. Alongside popular detective and soap formats, you'll find a wonderful pot-pourri of inventive and imaginative work: dramatised poems, drama-documentaries, 'devised' drama that is unscripted, and – coming to your radio sets soon (I write this in June 2005!) – a series of fast-turnaround plays which draw their inspiration specifically from recent events.

But our search for new talent is by no means limited to writing; many of Britain's finest actors started their career on radio, and will continue to do so. BBC schemes like the Carleton Hobbs bursary awards and the Norman Beaton Fellowship showcase new, exciting talent, while more established glitterati can be heard every week on Radios 3 and 4, BBC 7 and the World Service. As I look through this week's *Radio Times* there's an astonishing galaxy of talent on the airwaves; it's by no means an untypical radio broadcasting week, but if you listened to only half the dramatic output you could catch Janet McTeer, Victoria Hamilton, Penelope Wilton, Prunella Scales, Patricia Routledge, Anna Massey, Stephen Fry, David Calder, Emma Fielding, Adam Godley, Ian Hogg, Amanda Root, Joss Ackland, Frances Barber, Nickolas Grace, James Fleet, Patrick Barlow, Patrick Malahide, Sylvestra Le Touzel, Dougray Scott . . . and these are just names I've cherry-picked at random. Radio is an actor's medium as well as a writer's one; and I trust this book will enable more of you to, as it were, tread the airwaves.

Early in my radio directing career I auditioned, and then cast, a young actor straight from drama school, to play a small but important part in a radio version of Stoppard's *The Real Thing*. He gave a good performance, but I lost touch with him and never, unfortunately, worked with him again. I often wonder what happened to Ewan McGregor.

Gordon House
Head, BBC Radio Drama, April 2001–March 2005

Introduction

Radio is a unique medium making unique demands of the actor. For the listener the closest similar experience is reading a book, where the individual's imagination is called into play and the depth and vividness of what the listener and reader 'see' is determined by the quality of the writing or the acting. The minute the listener 'sees' the actor, script in hand, all illusion is lost and belief gone. There's a lot of fun to be had out of this medium but, more than in any other, conviction and commitment has to be total. If you cannot 'be it' totally, the listener will not 'see' you.

In real life there is a certain vocal messiness to interaction; years ago one could argue that radio acting was characterised by a formality in playing, a middle-class, impediment-free and resonant voice, beautifully spoken. Today, hopefully, such preconceptions are being eroded with a broad movement in favour of 'realness' – with whatever seeming vocal 'faults' or imperfections that contains.

Radio's other great strength is in its opportunities for actors of all shapes, sizes, ethnicity and styles. Released from the tyranny of the unchangeable look, actors often find that radio gives them at last the freedom to be themselves and to be able to express an aspect of the real person inside or, indeed, to be someone who is nothing like them!

There is a greater need than ever for actors to be versatile and none can ignore the employment possibilities of radio, with mainstream BBC outpouring attaining far larger audiences than theatre, and reaching international listeners through the World Service, while commissioning more new writing than any other medium outside of Hollywood. Radio drama has been penned the National Theatre of the Airwaves with good reason. Add to this the many independent radio producing companies, the talking book companies, the burgeoning CD-Rom market for actors' voices, the prolific – and lucrative – voice-over business, not to mention the documentary opportunities, and you can see why more actors than ever are looking for voice-over agents.

This is a book for actors, both new and those experienced but who have never got round to radio, students and teachers – and the material works equally well for TV and theatre practice. It will help you to prepare for audition and as a training tool. It is also practicable for technical students learning how to turn *sound* into *radio drama* – armed with these texts they can learn how to create sound pictures and learn how radio actors work.

The extracts are from contemporary plays – mirroring the mostly contemporary broadcast output. They offer challenging situations that exploit radio's special qualities and demands, giving the actor a chance to create effects and to make emotional contact with the microphone, the fellow actor and the listener. They all offer roughly equal parts for the two actors, with equal challenges and equal stories to play. They comprise a variety of styles, playing ages, ethnic backgrounds, accents, statuses: some are physically active, others still but intense; some give the actors the chance to create an atmosphere, as in the pub scene in *Two*, or a physical dilemma as in *Bedroom Farce.*

We hope that you go on to use our criteria when choosing scenes of your own. A duologue won't work where people are just talking aimlessly, where there is no emotional shape to the scene in terms of a beginning and ending, where the text requires the actor to shout, where the writing is overly sentimental or trite, or where the scene contains too much complicated action which confuses the listener and makes it hard for the actor to reach the microphone. It will work if there is a 'journey' involving a change in the characters' status, as will finding a scene where there is scope to create a life outside the text.

Once you have found a scene to work on you should look at the context of the scene within the whole play, where available. Your character choices need to be informed, and knowing what immediately precedes your scene – an action or a line of dialogue – helps create your opening objective by giving you an impulse, which is critical. Even if you don't source the play and the exact moment where this scene fits, make a choice for yourselves so that you have a clear reason to start the scene. Also, you may find other scenes within that play that better suit your requirements.

We are not going to take you through how to play a scene here – that is up to you and there are countless books written on the subject. The rules are the same for acting in all its forms. You will have made some basic decisions about what the scene is about, what objectives each character will play, maybe how they go about achieving those objectives. Truth, imagination, commitment and, most important, *listening* and *re-acting*, which is always the best sort of *acting*, are essential ingredients.

Radio*active* Warnings

In radio you have the script in front of you, so it can be difficult to remember to listen, not to just read; you might be anticipating your next lines or concentrating on coming in on cue, as opposed to focusing on what has just been said to you. The result can be actors reading lines in turn, which is neither truthful nor entertaining.

Another challenge lies in the lack of rehearsal time; the actor in radio might be tempted to make short cuts emotionally, to generalise. Scenes are usually shorter than in theatre, and the actor may feel the pressure to make an impact in little airtime. It is therefore crucial to make specific choices, to flesh out the inner life of the character sufficiently so that there are no clichés about the acting.

And finally, but most importantly, don't be tempted to concentrate on *your* voice rather than your character's thoughts as you speak. This can be very tempting, particularly if you do have a conventionally 'beautiful' voice, but it will not sound real, however much you might enjoy it!

We are going to take you through what are the *practical differences* for you within this medium.

- **Get the breathing right**. Whatever one is saying – in real life – is informed, breathwise, by what one is doing. We are never doing nothing, even listening, say, to a lecture, has a certain vocal quality. Try this out; think about how the breath is different if you have just walked into a room expecting to see one thing and actually see something else, or if you are having a chat in a nightclub – you may be adrenalised, you might pitch up; the breath always informs the acting and fills in the picture. But remember, it's not all about words on the page; it's also about the spaces between the words, literally so. A terminological plea! The 'pause' *develops* the scene; the 'silence' arrests it. The writer uses these two words for very different effect. Understand, play and enjoy the difference. A pause can be more eloquent than a line of text, a silence more telling than a whole monologue.
- Uniquely in this medium, you are creating the whole picture with your voice, so you have to keep the sound going by not holding your breath when you are not speaking. So, through the pauses and silences **the trick is to keep breathing**, as the saying goes. And the breathing should be audible but not in a manufactured way. The listener can enjoy impulses being vocalised on an in-breath, or a laugh under someone else's line. You're not 'live' only when you have a line, but for every second of the scene. Equally, you have to conjure the scenery, the costumes, the props, and all with nothing there physically, but everything there imaginatively; it stands to reason that if *you* don't see these things, the *listener* won't either.
- The microphone is the person(s) you are speaking to. You will need as much volume as would be required in real life to speak to a person that far from you. So **disengage the diaphragm**. Don't confuse intensity with volume; just talk to the person/microphone, don't project. This is probably the most common mistake made by actors starting in this medium, who are used to having to hit the back row with diaphragmatic support. The general sliding scale is as you build intensity so you decrease volume.

- **Play the microphone**. As you gain confidence with the notion that the person you are speaking to is the microphone, so you will develop a certain fluidity with it; though your feet may stay roughly in the same place during a scene, you could move your body subtly in and out during the dialogue, as in real life you might move in closer to say something that is more intimate, or move out as you release a laugh . . . play around with it; confident playing of the microphone makes for a more textured and interesting – and *real* – rendition of the scene. Listen to and play off your partner, make eye contact with the microphone, connect.
- **Syntax**. The punctuation, the exact words chosen and the order the words are placed in the sentence are not arbitrary. These are the very signals chosen by the writer to tell you everything you need to know about that character. If we assume that we are how we speak, it becomes crucial to follow to the letter the way your character speaks: that is who they are. The syntax is an exact mirror of the workings of that character's mind; it is their intellect. It might be worth going back to school books to determine what a semicolon means, as opposed to a colon, as opposed to a hyphen; some characters never finish sentences off . . . others talk in short, abrupt full stops. This all means something. Once you unlock the syntax, it reveals a rich inner seam to be mined by the more discerning actor!
- **Pick up the cues**. Radio plays faster than theatre. Listen and react. There should not be a gap between the listening and the line in reaction – in real life these are simultaneous. Go and actively eavesdrop on conversations. You will notice that the impulse to respond is taken midway through the previous line, not after it. Or, another example, if you want to study what real-life talking sounds like, try listening to someone speaking on the phone, to an unheard listener, which may be the closest thing to acting on radio. You will see and hear him take a breath to interrupt, hold it and wait, get interrupted himself, he will naturally raise his voice in places, sometimes listen, sometimes prepare what he wants to say next. Pace, volume and intensity

will vary, but at all times he is picturing the person on the other end of the line and he will react to what he is receiving back on many sensitive aural levels, exactly as the good actor will do at the microphone.

- **Spot**. In radio another person in the studio, known usually as the Spot Studio Manager, creates the sound that would be made by the actor in any other medium, like making a cup of tea, cleaning a window. The radio actor is holding a script so cannot always perform the required activity. Spot creates effects *on the spot* as opposed to those that are ambient and that would be added in the edit. Nevertheless, the actor has to breathe and energise the text as if actually creating the effect. If you look at the extract from *Duck* by Stella Feehily, you have a good illustration of this. Both characters are in the bath; he is washing her back, so how he breathes will be informed by that and how she receives the 'being washed' should also be evident. Spot would pour water, and splash about as if *they* are, and will take the lead from the actor. It is a creative, symbiotic and crucial relationship. So physicalise the performance. If you are washing a window in the scene, do it with your body and your breath, within the restrictions of holding a script.

- **Page-turning** is an art; every actor develops his own way to do this silently and without disrupting the emotional through line. That said, many directors now are fine about the actor making some noise at the end of each page, so long as this can be edited out cleanly and the actor doesn't lose fluidity within the scene. Practice makes perfect and to be seen at audition trying to turn silently shows professionalism.

Ages: We have stated the ages of the characters in the scene as indicated by the writers. The ages can be immaterial, for it is the dynamic within the playing of the status that is more eloquent and more interesting. Obviously it has to make sense, but there are scenes here where you can easily adjust the ages by several years and it would still stand up. Similarly, you may well be able to play someone older or younger than you, so don't dismiss any scene lightly. Each one offers a different acting challenge, and the creative possibilities are limitless. The joy of this medium is you can change everything about yourself, including age and even gender, although potential employers wouldn't usually want you to play much beyond your natural range, except in small parts to 'double up'. Actors who can convincingly play below eighteen are at a premium.

Accents: It will be obvious to you which scenes are written specifically for a certain accent, and we have indicated this too. If you are going to try an accent it has to be as good as 'native'. You may well get away with an accent onstage that you wouldn't on the radio. The listener is so much closer to your voice, any hesitation or inaccuracy is trebled. Equally, you can shift the terminology and colloquialism about so that it's possible to play the scene within an accent that works well for you. Be irreverent but authentic.

MC is ever-thankful to John Collis who runs the Learning Resources Centre at Rose Bruford College, which nourishes so many.

MLC is grateful for the help, encouragement and support of the Royal Welsh College of Music and Drama, particularly Judith Agus and Robert Edge, and Teresa Hennessy at the Drama Association of Wales Library.

The authors would like to thank Gordon House for writing the foreword and their families and loved ones for their forebearance!

This book is dedicated to all our students past and present who have taught us so much; to Patrick Edwards, *magnum opus* himself, who came up with the perfect title, and to Tal for her huge heart.

Art and Guff by Catherine Tregenna

Art and Guff, both mid thirties, Welsh accents.

Art and Guff are childhood friends from rural west Wales with one goal: to make it as writers by the time they are forty, or give up. Fast approaching their deadline, they have abandoned jobs and families to move to London in pursuit of their shared dream. Living off their giros, they keep up each other's morale with the determination to succeed, the will to escape obscurity and the enthusiastic grasping of whatever chances come their way. More like laddish teenagers than mature adults, they are happier thinking noble thoughts in the relative squalor of their bedsit, or going to the pub, than getting to grips with the task they've set themselves.

In this opening scene of the play, the two men arrive home from the pub in the early hours. Art is comfortably drunk and on a high, while Guff is weary, depressed and beginning to find Art's dissolute lifestyle and lack of focus irritating. Their differing pace and energy levels also show the polarity in their attitudes to achieving their ambition.

Their regional origins are quite specific – Kidwelly – therefore it's important to get the right Welsh accent, more so since it's written in the dialect. A Swansea accent would be a close approximation.

Art   Turn the light on, wuss. Guff?

He goes into the bathroom. There is a knock on the flat door. He calls out.

At this time of night!! Guff oh, get the door.

The knocking persists.

Guff? Get the bastard door, wuss. *Guff?*

Guff (*off*)   Art oh, let me in for fuck's sakes.

Art *comes out of the bathroom and opens the door.*

Guff   Donkey!

Art   Who came in with me then?

Guff   You nearly 'ad my nose off, mun.

Art   I could 'ave sworn . . .

Guff   I've noticed that about you, wuss. You never hold the door open or nothin'. Ego that is, see. And bad manners.

He looks in the mirror as **Art** *returns to the bathroom.*

Christ, I look more like my old man every day.

Art (*off*)   Good night though, wuss!

Guff   Crackin', dog's bollocks.

Art (*off*)   I'm on a high see, me. High on life.

Guff   Life and nine pints of Stella, innit?

Art (*off*)   Aye, drunk myself sober though see.

The toilet flushes. **Art** *emerges as* **Guff** *tries to take off his jacket.*

Hey, that club was alright.

Guff   Aye, bit loud though, wuss.

Art   See me dancin' tonight? Smooth I was. King of the Floor, me.

He picks up the remote control and flicks on the hi-fi. A 'Reef' CD – *'Place Your Hands' – plays loudly.*

Dance with me, wuss, I've got dancin' feet.

He grabs **Guff**'s *jacket sleeve. The jacket falls to the floor, small change scatters everywhere.* **Guff** *attempts to retrieve his coins.*

Guff Fuckin' hell, Art.

Art You said you 'ad no change for a cab. 'Pants on fire', Garfield Jones.

Guff I'm a bit peckish, wuss.

Art How come you never dance then?

Guff Stupid, mun. People jiggin' about in a little space.

Art You used to in school discos. I remember. Like this.

He takes awkward steps side to side, knocking each foot against his ankle in a slow rhythm – a laboured simpleton impression.

Kicking yourself in the shins, mun. You must have been black and blue for days after.

Pause.

Why did you dance like that, then?

Guff Bugger off.

Art Step, kick, step, kick.

Guff How about you tonight then? I don't think John Travolta'll be losin' any sleep over your moves, wuss. King of the Floor, my eye. Like a bastard windmill you were. You hit a woman in the face twice.

Art Oh aye. Step, kick . . . step, kick.

Guff Well, at least I only injure myself, innit?

The two face each other doing exaggerated impersonations of each other's dance styles. **Guff** *twists his arms wildly and shuffles his feet.* **Art** *steps and kicks.* **Guff** *stops.*

Aye, aye.

Art Step, kick, step, kick . . .

Guff   Aye, stop it now, wuss. It's/

Art/Guff (*together*)   /childish, mun.

Guff *stares at* **Art**.

Guff   Cut it out. *Cut it out, mun!*

Art   You hate it when I do that, don't you?

Guff   You . . . hate . . . it . . . don't you?

Guff *can't pull it off.*

Art   Look at you there trying to do it!

He collapses into uncontrollable laughter, hands on his knees.

The laughter turns into a racking cough. **Guff** *rises, goes into the kitchen area and pours a glass of water.* **Guff** *returns,* **Art** *holds out his hand. drinks it down.*

Aye, cheers, wuss.

Guff   Self-inflicted, innit? Smokin', mun. Cancer sticks. Don't get it, see. Never will. You're like a barrel of gravel, wuss. Never felt the need myself, see.

Art   Smug bugger.

Art *lights a cigarette.* **Guff** *waves away the smoke.*

Guff   Don't want to sleep in it, mun.

Art *turns the volume up on the hi-fi with the remote.*

Art   Don't hit me, wuss.

Guff   Give me that! Give! It's my fuckin' hi-fi so fuckin' hand it over, right?

They wrestle. **Art**, *laughing, holds the remote out of* **Guff**'s *reach.*

Give!

Art Alright, alright, don't get so proprietorial, mun!

He lets **Guff** *have it.* **Guff** *switches the hi-fi off and sits with the remote in his lap.*

You're so easy to wind up, aye.

Guff And you're a pain in the fuckin' arse.

Art I know. I'm sorry.

Guff Infant!

Art Weeble!

Guff Twat!

Art Here endeth *that* Battle of Wits.

Pause.

Hey, that bloke in the Crown. He was a few butties short of a picnic, aye.

Guff Thick as shit, mun.

Pause.

I can't believe you sold him your return ticket though.

Art (*cod Humphrey Bogart accent*) Sweetest twenty bucks a monkey ever made.

Guff You can't go home now though.

Art Couldn't anyway. It expired last week.

Guff Christ, mun. I should have sold him mine an' all.

Art One man makes but one journey, wuss.

Guff Why the fuck did he want to go to Kidwelly, anyhow?

Art   a) He's never been. b) It's got a castle and c) He's got sod all else to do.

Pause.

Oh yeah . . . and I told him Julie Christie lived there and drank in the White Horse on Wednesdays.

Guff (*contemplating the man's imminent disappointment*)   Shit.

Art   And the beauty of it is he'll never find out I lied cos the bastard ticket's expired! Genius, mun.

Guff   The words 'sand' and 'Arab' spring to mind.

Art   You want to watch that.

Guff   Toast?

Art   To who?

Guff   Toast, mun. D'you want some?

Art   No, can't be bothered.

Beautiful Thing by Jonathan Harvey

Jamie, fifteen; Ste, sixteen; London accents.

Sandra lives alone with her teenage son Jamie in a block of flats on a south-east London estate. They have a friendly relationship with Ste, who lives next door with his bullying brother and father. Ste is a frequent visitor, usually escaping from the tyranny of his family.

In this scene, Ste has accepted Sandra's invitation to stay the night after a particularly violent row with his father. The flat is small and he must share Jamie's bed 'top to tail'.

Ste is only a year older, but considerably more mature than Jamie, who is impressionable and lacking a sound and regular male influence in his life. Ste's relative popularity and athleticism contrast with Jamie's feelings of isolation at school and his reluctance to take part in sporting activities. There should be no sense whatever of a seduction by either character, although the unspoken plays a strong part in the scene. An excellent opportunity for working in stereo.

Ste   You don't mind?

Jamie   No.

Ste   You sure?

Jamie   Course.

Ste   I could sleep on the floor.

Jamie   You hate the floor.

Ste   And you don't mind?

Jamie   No. I don't.

Ste   Great.

Ste *lays the salad on the bed and sits on the bed to undress. During the following he begins to undress for bed.*

Jamie   Haven't you eaten?

Ste   No. It's not yours, is it?

Jamie   No. Do you want the light off?

Ste   Do you?

Jamie   Don't care.

Ste   D'you mind it on?

Jamie   No.

Ste   Coz o'the salad.

Jamie   Fine.

Ste *is taking his shirt off now. Then his trousers follow.*

Jamie   Mum went really mad at me today. This games business. She threw a load of me old stuff out I was hangin' on to.

Ste   Yeah?

Jamie   Yeah.

Pause. **Ste** *now has his boxer shorts on.*

Jamie   D'you want another T-shirt?

Ste   Nah, I'm all right, Jay.

Jamie   Are you sure?

Ste   Sure.

Jamie   Well, if you do.

Ste   Cheers. I'm getting in now.

Jamie   Right.

Ste *gets into bed. His head the opposite end to* **Jamie**. **Jamie** *passes him a pillow.*

Jamie   Have this.

Ste   Cheers.

He puts the pillow behind him and sits up. He makes a start on the salad.

D'you mind me eating this?

Jamie   Nah. I was gonna read anyway.

Ste   What you readin' then?

Jamie   Er . . . it's me mum's. (*Holds magazine up.*)

Ste   Oh yeah? I've seen that in the shop. (*Notices it's called* Hello!) Hello!

Jamie   Hello!

They have a bit of a giggle about this.

'Ere, d'you wanna fork?

Ste   Nah, eat it with me fingers.

Jamie   Want some bread?

Ste   This is great.

Jamie   Right. (*Pause.*) I'm gonna read now.

Ste   Okay.

Silence. **Jamie** *casually reads the magazine,* **Ste** *munches on the salad.*

Cor, I'm starving.

Jamie   Can't have you goin' hungry, can we?

Ste   What bit you reading?

Jamie   It's about Sally from *Coronation Street.*

Ste   What, the blonde one?

Jamie   Yeah.

Ste   What's it say then?

Jamie   (*reads*) Although Sally spends her working week filming in Manchester, she likes nothing better than to spend her weekends at her London penthouse flat. Weekends are busy for Sally, juggling a hectic social life with time for that special man in her life. Her partner is another actor, but she is coy about revealing his name. Saturdays are spent shopping and eating out, and Sundays are set aside for catching up with old friends or taking long strolls on Hampstead Heath which her flat overlooks.

Pause.

Ste   That's north of the river, innit?

Jamie   Mm.

Ste   So she's called Sally? In real life as well as on the telly?

Jamie   Yeah, I hate that name.

Ste   It's not her fault I s'pose.

Jamie   I blame the parents.

Ste   Mm. D'you always wear glasses when you read?

Jamie   Supposed to.

Ste   You don't in school.

Jamie   Hardly fetching, is it?

Ste   Nah, looks all right.

Jamie   Yeah?

Ste Yeah, I'm telling ya.

Jamie How's your salad?

Ste Bang on food.

Jamie Good for your sports.

Ste That's right. Good for your spots an' all.

Jamie You haven't got any spots.

Ste Yours are clearing up.

Jamie Tar.

Ste D'you fancy that Sally?

Jamie Not really. Do you?

Ste Nah. Haven't given it much thought.

Jamie D'you fancy her next door?

Ste Fancy Leah?

Jamie She fancies you.

Ste Don't.

Jamie I'm only saying.

Ste Jamie.

Jamie What time should I set the alarm for?

Ste Quarter to eight.

Jamie Right. (*He gets alarm clock off the floor. Whilst setting it.*) If you wanna bath in the morning I can put the water on.

Ste Nah, I'll get home.

Jamie Right.

Ste   Jamie?

Jamie   What?

Ste   Will your mum mind if I leave this beetroot?

Jamie   No.

Ste   Only she asked if I liked it.

Jamie   Leave it if you don't wannit.

Ste   She won't mind?

Jamie   No. She's not a very good cook, my mum.

Ste   She is.

Jamie   Hmm, that's a matter of opinion.

Ste *puts the plate on the floor and starts to settle down in the bed.*

Jamie   You goin' sleep?

Ste   Yeah, I'm knackered.

Jamie   I'll turn the light off.

He puts the magazine on the floor and turns off the bedside lamp. He settles down. Silence.

Ste?

Ste   Mm?

Jamie   You all right?

Ste   Yeah.

Jamie   Right. (*Pause.*) Ste?

Ste   What?

Jamie   I thought you were making the tea tonight?

Ste   I burnt it.

Jamie   Oh.

Ste   Mm.

Jamie   What was it?

Ste   Bubble and squeak.

Jamie   Oh yeah. (*Pause.*) Ste?

Ste   What?

Jamie   Night.

Ste   Night, Jamie.

Silence.

Been So Long by Che Walker

Gil, twenty; Barney, forties; London accents.

Set in a Camden bar in 1998, this play sums up the vibe in
north London's underclass of young people without much
in their lives other than disillusion, poverty and mistrust.

Here, in the opening scene, Gil, a volatile man with a
heightened sense of injustice, is looking for Raymond. He
wants to kill him, for reasons which become evident in the
scene. Now, Raymond is a mythical figure in this world,
beautiful, dangerous, a man who can and who does take a
different woman home every night. He is amoral. Barney is
the sort of guy who can be in a room but be invisible. He
disappears and reappears without a sound. Barney has seen
everything, has worked in bars for ever, and has been
working in this bar since it knew better days, though now it
is an empty failure of a joint. Somerstown is a particularly
rough part of Camden.

Barney   Evening.

Pause.

What would you like to drink?

Gil   Don't like the way you asked me that question.

Pause.

Barney   I see.

Gil   Something 'boutchour tone.

Pause.

Barney   Something about my tone . . .

Gil   How long you worked this gig?

Barney   In this bar, or bars in general?

Gil   Yes.

Barney   Which one?

Gil   Both. Wanna know all of it.

Barney   Four years here, ten years in all.

Gil   You're burnt out.

Barney   I don't feel burnt out.

Gil   Burnt out, mate. This place smells funny.

Barney   Any movement on your choice of drink?

Gil   Heard you was closing down.

Barney   Next month.

Gil   No . . .

Barney   Jake's across the road has killed us.

Gil   Jake's, right, I passed that gaff on the way up here. Place was ramup. All the pretty people from MTV.

Barney   MTV mob used to chance it in here. Can only surmise it got a little too rough for them.

Gil   Packed over there. Both floors.

Barney   Yeah.

Gil   Jake and his brothers know how to run a party.

Barney   I'd work there if they had a position for me.

Gil   What about your punters?

Barney   My punters are mostly in Jake's.

Pause. **Gil** *breathes deeply.*

Gil It's time. Yes. Yes. It's time.

Barney I beg your pardon?

Gil Taste it, Gil, taste it, mate.

Barney You getting ready to order a drink?

Gil SHUTCHOUR MOUTH!

Pause.

Where is he?

Barney Where is who?

Gil Raymond LeGendre.

Barney Who?

Gil Raymond LeGendre.

Barney Raymond LeGendre . . . Don't know nobody called Raymond LeGendre.

Gil *grabs* **Barney** *and slams his head on the counter. He smashes an empty beer bottle and holds it close to* **Barney**'s *neck.*

Gil I'M NOT HERE TO BE FUCKED ABOUT! IT IS TIME! I WILL BE DENIED NO LONGER! I'VE TRAINED LONG AND HARD FOR WHAT I'M GONNA DO TO RAYMOND LE FUCKING GENDRE! IT IS MY DESTINY TO FILLET THE MAN! I HAVE SPENT THREE LONG YEARS OF MY LIFE TURNING MYSELF INTO A SHARK THAT BREATHES! (*Suddenly quiet.*) Again I ask you: where is Raymond LeGendre?

Barney (*his face squashed*) I hnstly dnt knw th gzr.

Gil You're a big fat fucking liar!

Gil *releases* **Barney**.

Barney Perhaps if you described the fella. Wha's he look like?

Gil   Raymond LeGendre?

Pause.

He looks good, man. Tall man. Powerful physique. Moves easy. Athletic. Crisp garms. Birds go potty for him. He's relaxed, you see? They feel safe. He makes 'em laugh, he's cheeky. Like a kid, makes 'em giggle and drop their drawbridge. Perfect pitch. He must die.

Barney   Wait a minute . . . I know who you mean. Used to box a little in that gym across from the Talacre?

Gil   That's the one. Geezer keeps hisself well trim.

Barney   Used to come here every night, back when we was booming. Zoomed right in on the women. Could set your clock by him pulling. You'd know it was time for last orders when he'd be helping a girl on with her coat. Every night. Different girl, same result.

Gil   Definitely the same cat.

Barney   Geezer should be in movies or summink.

Gil   Geezer should be neutered. Where is he? Raymond LeGendre.

Barney   On my life, mate, if it's the same guy, he's not stepped in here for two years at least. I don't know if he moved out the area, or got religion or got married or what, but he's not been in here for two years, I swear.

Gil   If you're blowing smoke up my arse, I'll gut you Somerstown style.

Barney   Got no reason to protect him, don't know the man. Just used to watch him work the women every night.

Pause.

Gil   Some geezers go through life . . . I dunno, they just, they just, they just . . . Flow, y'know? Glide through it. Fluid. Effortless. Pain-free. No fear, no sweat . . .

And some geezers go through life . . . They bounce into one brick wall after another. 'Til they're fucking blind with brain damage . . . And they know, after a while, they know . . . what their lot is gonna be . . . Then they start to smell bad.

Pause.

Listen, my friend. I'm sorry, I put my hands on you. Y'wanna bar, bar me. I'm a wrong 'un. I'm a wrong 'un.

Barney   Forget about it.

Gil   Been trying to forget about it for three years. Have a drink wimme.

Barney   You pour. My hands are still shaking.

Barney *puts out a whisky bottle and two short glasses.* **Gil** *puts some money on the counter and pours the drinks.*

Gil   Cheers.

Barney   Cheers.

Gil   Gil.

Barney   Barney.

Gil   Easy.

Barney   Niceness.

Pause.

Gil   Ain'tcha curious as to why I wanna kill Raymond LeGendre?

Barney   Not remotely.

Pause. **Gil** *breaks down crying,*

Gil   He took my girl from me.
He took my girl,
He took my girl,

He took my girl,
He took my fucking girl from me.
Any girl he wanted, he took my girl.
I only had the one girl . . .
Both of 'em, both of 'em laughin' at me.
I couldn't be more humiliated if I'd shat meself in public.
Raymond Le Gendre . . . He took the love from me.

Barney *hands* **Gil** *a tissue.*

Burn the Aeneid! by Martyn Wade

Varius and Tucca, any age, any accent.

Set in 19 BC, the poet Virgil has just died, leaving his great work the *Aeneid* unfinished. In a codicil in his will he left instructions for it to be destroyed, as it was so much less than perfect. He also spoke this wish out loud.

However, his literary executors Marcus Tucca and Lucius Varius (and dog Homer makes three) cannot bear to destroy it. Against all the odds they fight to keep it in the world – Varius even has to sleep with Drusilla, the wife of Virgil's half-brother, the main benefactor of the will, to encourage her support in the business. She is now in love with him, love which is far from reciprocated. When a literary rival insists that Virgil's wishes be obeyed in law all seems lost. Then, at the eleventh hour, the Emperor sends an envoy, ensuring that the work is immediately returned to Rome for safe keeping and for posterity. Tucca and Varius, engaged as editors, rush back to their hotel room, thrilled, only to meet with disaster.

*The corridor outside **Virgil***'s suite.*

Varius (*elated, but trying to keep his voice down*) Tucca, my Tucca!

He kisses him enthusiastically, and they begin to go down the corridor.

Tucca Rooms and facilities provided by the Emperor . . .

Varius Hee, hee! Regular salary for the period of the editing itself.

Tucca And, and . . . a lump sum –

Varius A lump sum!

Tucca On satisfactory completion. Did you see his face?

Varius Mucius?

Tucca So drained of blood it was almost translucent.

They come to a stop outside their own suite.

His eyes . . . (*Searching for the key.*) Have I got the key? (*Finding it.*) Yes. Eyes staring like a madman's. (*Unlocking the door and opening it.*) Mouth (*trailing off*) worldlessly opening and shutting . . .

Varius *and* **Tucca***'s suite – the main room.* **Tucca** *enters.*

Tucca *utters a shriek of agony.*

Varius (*from outside*)   Marcus – I'm not coming in. And I don't want to know what's happened.

Tucca *sobs.*

Varius Please, Jupiter, whatever it is – don't let it be to do with the *Aeneid*.

Tucca (*in between sobs*)   It's something to do with the *Aeneid*.

Varius It's been stolen.

Tucca No – I suspect not.

Varius Thank you, Jupiter.

Tucca Eaten. By and large. Look!

Varius Thank you, blessed Jove. Thank you! (*Pause.*) Eaten! (*Entering.*) Eaten? By Homer?

Tucca No, Lucius – the chambermaid.

Varius Who had it last? Who left it sitting out? It was you, you fool! Oh! Oh!

Beat.

What's this? (*Picking up a small piece of paper, and reading.*) 'And protesting fled to the shadows below. *Finis.*' So that's how it ends. Oh!

Tucca   Oh!

They mourn the Aeneid.

Tucca (*whistles*)   Homer!

Varius   What are you doing?

Tucca   I'm calling your dog. He's got to be punished.

Varius   Don't be absurd, Tucca. Homer's far too smart to fall for that one. Where is he, anyway?

Tucca   Under the settee. I'm going to beat him within an inch of his life. No – I'm not going to be that accurate. Homer! (*He whistles again.*)

Varius   See? He's not coming.

Tucca   Yes. But that's not because he's smart. It's because he's stupid.

Varius   Well, if he's that stupid, why bother calling him? (*Pause.*) You're not going to kill him, Tucca.

Tucca   I think I am, actually.

Varius   Over my dead body.

Tucca   Very well. I'm going to kill you first and then I'll kill the dog. And then I'll kill myself. Oh! (*He sobs.*)

Varius *sobs.*

Varius   Come on, Marcus. Let's collect all these little pieces up. *Nil desperandum.* (*Picking up a piece, and reading it.*) 'Our only hope is in ourselves.' (*Taking encouragement from this.*) That's true, Publius Vergilius. (*Reading on.*) 'And it's a slight hope, as you see.' (*Less* *encouraged.*) That's true, too. Very true. Such a helpful book, the *Aeneid.*

Tucca You're mad. We can't present the Emperor with an epic in thirty fragments.

Varius (*picking up another piece*) What's this bit? (*Reading.*) 'You must go on; tread boldly where the path will take you.' Thank you very much, Publius. Of course, some parts might still be undigested. When Homer next goes for poo poo . . .

Tucca Oh right. And in case there's still a few other lines of verse waiting in there for the light of day, I'll open Homer up, and read the entrails.

Varius (*severely*) Tucca.

Tucca We've had it, Lucius. All over. Time to fall on our swords.

Varius You're not serious. (*Relieved.*) Of course you're not. We don't have any swords.

Tucca We'll slash our veins. Drown in the bath. Throttle each other.

Varius (*pretending to consider the options*) No. Not really happy with any of those . . .

Tucca But to go on living . . . To face the Emperor's wrath . . . (*Going towards the window.*) What about jumping from the window and smashing our skulls? (*Opening the window.*) It's not far enough down, though. We'd survive – and everyone would think we'd been trying to run away.

Varius Oh, how ignominious. (*Joining* **Tucca** *at the window.*) Why don't we do that? Run away, I mean.

Tucca Varius – you sheep-heart! (*Warming to the idea.*) With one bound, we're free. Free of the *Aeneid.*

Varius Free of Drusilla.

Tucca We'll change our identities.

Varius Start our lives all over again. Be *really* successful this time.

Tucca But we'll still be . . . ?

Varius Chums? Oh yes.

Tucca Well . . . ready?

Varius Yes. No! What about Homer?

Tucca He can change his identity too.

Varius He has to come with us. (*Calling him.*) Homer! Tell him he's been forgiven.

Tucca Never!

Varius He'll not come out otherwise.

Tucca (*to* **Homer**) You're forgiven, you odious mutt.

Homer *emerges from behind the settee.*

Varius Good boy.

Tucca Bad boy.

Varius Come here.

Homer *approaches* **Varius** *with a happy bark.*

Varius He's sorry, he says, and he won't do it again.

Tucca That's true enough.

Varius I suppose, really, we should get Probus in. Dictate a codicil or two, just in case anything goes wrong with our jump. You could give me an instruction to burn your books.

Tucca That's assuming I make you my literary executor.

Varius   Hoity-toity. No – we'll not bother with the legal stuff. Life's too short. Here we go then. A bold, imaginative leap through the window of opportunity.

All three get on to the window ledge. Traffic and people down below.

Varius   I count one, two, three, and then we each shout out, to encourage ourselves, and then –

Tucca (*nervous*)   It's an awfully –

Varius   No, Marcus. It's not a long way down. You said so yourself. Happy?

Tucca   Not exactly.

Varius   One, two, three . . . (*He produces a feeble shout.*)

Tucca *likewise.*

Homer *barks.*

Tucca (*after a slight pause*)   I knew you didn't have what it takes. I'd have gone, but I was sure you wouldn't, so I decided not to.

Dogs Barking by Richard Zajdlic

Neil and Ray, both early thirties, any accent.

Following a fling with his boss, Neil's relationship with Alex
has ended, but now he's regretting leaving both the flat and
the girlfriend, and he attempts, by devious and flagrant
means, to claim half-ownership of the property. He gains
access, and while Alex is out he tries to stake his claim – and
in so doing prove he has the upper hand – by removing all
her belongings.

For this he enlists the help of his frequently exploited
friend and van owner, Splodge (Ray), by concealing his
intentions and inventing a reconciliation with Alex. The
naive and good-hearted Ray has himself been ousted from
his marital home and is currently dogged by the Child
Support Agency. He is used to Neil's manipulations, but he
has a soft spot for Alex and doesn't feel comfortable about
Neil's plan, which sounds pretty suspicious to him, and
anyway, he's damaged his knee playing football . . .

Neil thinks that his loyal and dimwitted friend will
obediently obey his wishes. However, he has reckoned
without Ray's reluctance to be fobbed off and his superior
knowledge of Alex's current love life, which acts as the
turning point in this particular battle of wills.

Ray What are you doing?

Neil Just shifting some stuff. You don't mind, do you?

Ray Eh?

Neil Taking them with you. It's just these and the trunk. I thought
we could stash them at your Mum's place. In the garage. That's not
a problem, is it?

Neil *puts the cases down and goes to the kitchen to get out a number of plastic carrier bags.*

Ray Well, I don't know.

Neil It's only temporary – 'til we get ourselves a bit settled.

Ray What's in them?

Neil Clothes mainly. Bits and pieces. Thought we'd best have a clear-out. Get rid of all the crap. Won't be room for any of my stuff otherwise.

Ray I can't help with the carrying –

Neil Yes, I've realised that. 'S okay. I need you up here anyway. Buzz me back in.

Ray Ain't you got a key?

Neil Not yet, no. Alex changed the locks, didn't she?

Ray *nods, confused. He watches as* **Neil** *takes a plastic bag and starts to clear the shelf unit of* **Alex**'s *collection of china animals and assorted bric-a-brac.*

Ray She out then, is she? Alex.

Neil That's right.

Ray Bit of a turn-up, innit? Taking you back.

Neil More inevitable really.

Ray I thought you were with that Caroline bird?

Neil Not for a while now. Got a bit clingy, you know?

Ray You mean, she dumped you? (*Laughs.*) You should have brought her down the club. Introduce her to some real men.

Neil *laughs, despite himself.*

Ray   We never did get to meet her though, did we?

Neil   Other way round, I think.

Ray   She can't have been that ugly. You wouldn't have passed up Alex for some sweaty old Doris, would you?

Neil   *dumps the loaded bag into the trunk, opening another to continue.*

Neil   What about you? You getting it out much? Aside from to piss with, I mean.

Ray   Oh, you know. Have me moments. I've got a housewife in Brentford looks possible.

Neil   Still fitting, yes?

Ray   Fucking nightmare it is. She's having a kitchen in the Wolsey traditional, burgundy red. It's gonna suck all the light in, make the place look even pokier than it is. Should've had it in pastels at least, try and lift it up out of itself . . . what?

Neil (*grinning*)   Nothing.

Ray   'S not funny. If she ain't satisfied she'll complain to the company. I ain't staff any more. 'S all short-term contracts now, innit? Fuck up once and you're out.

Neil   Well, make sure she is satisfied.

He holds his hand out, palm up and waggles his middle finger in a sexual gesture.

Ray (*laughs*)   Yeah. I could, couldn't I? (*Beat.*) Not getting the signs though, you know? I think she's just being friendly.

Neil *dumps the second bag into the trunk and crosses to the stereo unit to start packing* **Alex***'s record and CD collection into another bag.*

Neil   What sort of friendly?

Ray   Cups of tea. Bit of cake. Just chatting really.

He watches **Neil** *pack, increasingly troubled.*

You chucking them out as well?

Neil   Everything. Have a look through them if you like. See if there's anything you fancy.

Ray (*uncertain*)   Yeah, I will. Ta.

Neil   Same with the clothes. You find a bra your size, you take it – no questions asked.

Ray (*laughs*)   Yeah, you'd like me in that, wouldn't you? You fucking perv.

Neil   You'll try one on, don't pretend otherwise.

Ray   Nah. I go for the panties, me. Nothing like a bit of snatch cloth to get you going, eh? (*Sniffs. Laughs.*) No offence.

Neil *starts filling a second bag.* **Ray** *broods on the curiousness of it all.*

Ray   So, when'd all this happen then? With Alex.

Neil   Last night.

Ray   Yeah? What? You just turned up and . . .

Neil   Pretty much.

Ray   No, go on, what? What d'you say to her?

Neil   I don't know. We just talked. Bottle of wine. Went to bed.

Ray *thinks about that.* **Neil** *continues packing.*

Ray   D'you fuck her?

Neil   What?

Ray   Did you?

Neil *laughs and takes the two bags of CDs/cassettes over to the trunk.*

Ray   What? What's wrong with that? I want to know. Did you have sexual intercourse? You did, didn't you? I bet you were fucking like dogs all night. Eh?

Ray *does a very vocal re-enactment of the supposed frenzied action.* **Neil** *is scanning the room for other things to pack. He stops, studying* **Ray** *not unsympathetically.*

Neil   It's been quite a while for you, hasn't it, Splodge?

Ray   I can't tell you. I'd have you if you bent over long enough.

Neil *laughs and moves to start taking down the pictures on the walls: glass-framed and Blu-Tacked posters alike.* **Ray** *watches, very troubled. He stands and goes to get himself some chocolate.* **Neil** *strips the walls.*

Ray   Look, I ain't being funny, right?

Neil   Okay.

Ray   But, she does know about this, don't she? I mean, Alex. She does know what you're doing here.

Neil   Yes, of course. Why?

Ray   'S a bit wholesale, innit?

Neil   We're making a fresh start. New beginning, see? It was her idea. Get everything out. Build it up again from scratch. Left me to do it all, of course, while she goes shopping (*Laughs.*) So not that fucking new, eh?

Silence. **Neil** *removes pictures.* **Ray** *drinks lager, eats chocolate.*

Ray   I heard she was seeing someone.

Neil   Ben Morris?

Ray   I don't know –

Neil   That's who I heard it was. Who did you hear?

Ray   No one particular. Just that she was –

Neil   It's Ben Morris.

Ray   Oh right. Who is he?

Neil   Friend of mine. You don't know him.

Neil *takes the pictures back to the trunk.* **Ray** *considers the new information.*

Ray   Well, okay. Him then. What's happening with that?

Neil   Not my problem, is it?

He packs the pictures, a little roughly. He stops, brooding angrily.

She was screwing him before we split up. D'you know that? (*Scoffs.*) Sounds familiar, doesn't it?

He continues packing, then starts to close the trunk, fasten the clasps.

Neil   Where are you parked? Round the back?

Ray   Side. Liskin Street.

Neil   Give us the keys then.

Ray *thinks about that as* **Neil** *checks his watch again and gets up.*

Neil   Splodge? Keys?

Other People by Christopher Shinn

Stephen and Mark, both mid twenties, American accents.

Mark is Stephen's ex-boyfriend and he is staying for a while in the apartment Stephen shares with Petra – on the sofa – having had a nervous breakdown six months previously. Stephen is an aspiring playwright. Mark has just had phenomenal success as a screenwriter; he is also a recovering alcoholic who has been sober since the breakdown, and he has found God in rehab. His life now seems to be far from the drug-induced haze it once was – he is even celibate.

He recently picked up a young down-and-out, Tan, helping him out by letting him shower at the apartment, eat, borrow clothes, nothing more. Stephen has not judged any of Mark's quite bizarre behaviour at this stage; he is a true friend accepting everything that comes with the new Mark. Stephen is chatty, loving and supportive, and however much he still loves Mark, he is giving him all the space he needs to recover. This scene marks the turning point in the equilibrium, and the beginning of a regression in Mark's behaviour.

As Stephen suddenly walks in, Mark puts down the phone. Stephen discovers later in the scene it was a phone sex line.

Stephen Hey sweets!

Mark Hi.

Stephen Merry Christmas Eve. How are you?

Mark I'm fine. How are you?

Stephen Ugh shopping is *done*!

Mark   Good day?

Stephen   Great day! You?

Mark   Okay.

Stephen   How's Tan?

Mark   He hasn't come by.

Stephen   Oh? I hope he's all right.

Mark   Me too.

Stephen   So are you all ready for Christmas Eve?

Mark   Yes.

Stephen   Are you going to church?

Mark   Tomorrow morning.

Stephen   Oh, maybe I can go with you.

Mark   I don't think that's appropriate.

Stephen   Oh?

Mark   My faith is very special to me. I take it very seriously.

Stephen   Well – I'm not going to sit there making pedophile jokes about the priest.

Mark   I'm sorry. You understand.

Stephen   Well. Okay, whatever you need. I bumped into Petra at the deli, she'll be here in a couple of minutes.

He goes into his room, takes stuff out of the bags.

So were you on the phone with Hollywood?

Mark   When?

Stephen   When I came in. You were on the phone.

Mark No, I was thinking of calling someone.

Stephen Oh. Hey, did you get the mail?

Mark Yeah, you didn't get anything.

Stephen Fuck.

Mark I got something.

Stephen Yeah?

Mark They sent me the cut of the movie.

Stephen *re-enters the living room. Sees the large envelope atop the VCR.*

Stephen The – your movie?

Mark I need to make a decision by – it's going to be at Sundance – so they need to know. If I want. My name on it. I haven't – watched it yet.

Stephen Wow . . . well, I'm sure that's going to be difficult for you.

Mark What do you care about Tan?

Beat.

Stephen Excuse me?

Mark When you came in. 'How's Tan?'

Stephen Are we all right here?

Mark I mean just let me live my life don't. Judge me all the time.

Stephen O-kay . . . is there . . . something you'd like to talk about?

Mark How's Tan, Who were you on the phone with, I mean. Just – no – exactly – there is nothing about all this I'd like to talk to you about as long as you're *judging* me –

Stephen All right, wait a second –

Mark Your rage is so transparent and it's just toxic, you know, it's poisoning this whole –

Stephen Rage?

Mark Yes, rage, at me, yes. I'm sorry we're not having sex, I'm sorry this is so upsetting to you.

Stephen *Mark?*

Mark 'How's Tan?'

Stephen Okay, okay I'm not going to yell and, and also it's Christmas Eve, but what I will say, what I will say is that you're, you're really – hurting my feelings here. Okay? So just – so just be a human being here for a second and let's go back to –

Mark *What?*

Stephen What? What?

Mark What, I don't know how to be a human being now?

Stephen That's not what I said.

Mark What did you say then?

Stephen Okay, let's take deep breaths –

Mark Can you SHUT UP for a second? you're always fucking TALKING.

Stephen Shut – Mark – what – I ask how you are, I ask about your life – you know if anyone should be angry here – Jesus Fucking Christ! –

Mark Oh, thank you.

Stephen Oh, *oh,* excuse me for taking the fucking Lord's name in vain, I'm sorry I'm not SPIRITUAL like you taking you know fucking becoming intimate with a fucking STREET KID hustler drug dealer whatever and you can't, you can't even fucking find ten MINUTES to talk to me –

Mark   Stop yelling!

Stephen   Stop – no! – you don't, you don't ask to even read what I'm working on, you sit here all day, *my* house, you invite this *kid* –

Mark   So you're jealous, because you think, you have some *idea* –

Stephen   Well I'm sorry if I'm a little fucking cynical I mean where's, how are you being a good Christian all this religious BULLSHIT, I mean, go fucking pass out food to smelly ugly homeless men, don't give me this Christian shit about – being –

Mark   Stop yelling!

Stephen   – no, go deliver food to people dying of AIDS, go, fuck you –

Mark   STOP YELLING!

Pause. **Mark** *beginning to cry.*

Stephen   Oh – come on – don't – don't – why are you – don't cry –

Mark   You know I was – I was – away for a long time I wasn't in the world and – I'm *adjusting* you know and it's not – I'm doing the best I – it's hard and you could show some – compassion –

Stephen   Come on, don't cry –

Mark   – because – I just wanted – a safe space and – you fucking accuse me of – all this judging, all this – let he who is without sin cast the first – you know? – I never said I was – perfect and I'm sorry if I'm not who – you wanted – me – to be – anymore –

Stephen   No, that's not – come on, don't cry. That's not it. I'm sorry, I shouldn't have – yelled I.

Mark *breaks down.* **Stephen** *puts his arm around him.*

Stephen   I just – if you're in pain I want to – it's – shhhh, come on. Shhh. It's okay. Shhh.

Some Voices by Joe Penhall

Ray, early twenties; Pete, early thirties; London accents.

Ray has battled schizophrenia for many years; he has recently been released from hospital, on the understanding that he is supervised and lives with his brother Pete. Their family history (Mother died of cancer years ago, Father, also dead, was an alcoholic who lost everything) is such that Pete is very much the carer in this relationship, he is the grounded one. But Ray can still outsmart his brother: he's failing to take his medication, has formed a relationship with a pregnant woman, been beaten up by her boyfriend in the process and has started drinking again.

Now, Ray has brought Ives, his friend from the hospital, to Pete's home in Shepherds Bush (the Bush) and told Ives that he can stay there, without asking his brother. Ives is seriously disturbed and Pete has enough to do looking after Ray; he has just sent Ives away and the two brothers are left alone.

Pete *sighs and sits at the table. Pause.*

Pete   You know, Ray . . . if you wanna piss your life away then fine but don't piss mine away too. You . . . see what I'm saying?

Pause. **Ray** *sits at the table.* **Pete** *picks up a can from the table, crushes it and throws it back.*

Pete   This is just what dad used to do.

Ray   Is it now.

Pete   That's how he pissed his caff away, pissed it all away drinking.

Ray   He was a drunk. That's what drunks do.

Pete   You never went through with him what I went through. Is that how you wanna end up? Is it?

Pause. **Pete** *pulls out the phial of pills from his pocket and plonks them on the table.* **Ray** *grabs them.*

Ray   I been looking for those everywhere.

Pete   Do I have to stand over you morning and night every night for the rest of your life? (*Beat.*) For the rest of your life, Ray.

Ray *shrugs.*

Pete   And . . . for the rest of my life. I mean how weird are things gonna get? You been out two weeks and you haven't done any of the things you're supposed to do. I'm keeping my end of the deal what about yours?

Ray   Don't talk to me about deals – I'm not doing any more deals.

Pete   You want me to force you, is that it?

Ray   How you gonna force me?

Pete   I don't know, Ray. I'm sure I'll think of something.

Ray   Drugs are bad for you, Pete. Everybody knows that.

Pete   Not these ones! Jesus.

Ray   They lead to worser things.

Pete   Oh, like what? Like . . . him? Do you wanna end up under a bridge as well?

Ray   I'm weaning myself off 'em.

Pete   What?

Ray Going for a more natural approach. I need a whatisit . . .
stable environment. Need to be around people I know and can trust
and all that.

Pete But you never are around, Ray, I never know where you are!
Where do you go? Where have you . . . Where have you been?

Ray With Laura. I told you.

Pete Oh, don't start that again.

Ray 'Don't start'? Don't start what again?

Beat.

You still don't believe me, do you?

Beat.

I'm tired of living here.

Pete Why?

Ray You got noisy neighbours. Every damn night I hear them
revving up their fancy cars and popping champagne corks. What's
the matter, Pete, you grown out of the Bush? You in a different
bracket now so you don't notice things any more?

Pete What am I supposed to notice?

Ray These . . . *arseholes.* I've seen them trotting about in their
tennis outfits with their dolly birds with the sunbed tans. I've seen
them go where the sunbeds are and come back orange. They're
probably all your customers. It's disgusting. What I need is a gun, a
Sten gun, that'd put a few holes in their party frocks.

Pause.

Pete Jesus, Ray, they're only –

Ray Fuckers.

Pete They're my neighbours.

Ray It's doing my head in.

Pete They're just people.

Ray People do my head in.

Pause.

Pete You mean . . . 'doing your head in' or actually doing your head in?

Ray I mean it gets on my tits.

Pete Well, Ray, you don't have to live here. You don't have to do any of this. Nor do I. I mean . . . (*Beat.*) Maybe you could get your own place. Bedsit or something. That's the idea, isn't it? Get you on your own two feet. (*Beat.*) I mean they can't expect you to stay here for ever. Can they?

Ray I'm going to Laura's.

Pete Are you now.

Ray Yeh.

Pete Oh well, Jesus, why the hell not – you been going out with her for a whole two weeks. Good idea.

Beat.

You're serious, aren't you? There really is a Laura?

Ray Yeh.

Pete And that's where you been staying?

Ray What's wrong with that?

Pete (*beat*) OK, well then, maybe we should do something. (*Beat.*) Talk to them about it. (*Beat.*) We'll go in there and tell 'em there's a change in plan. Fuck their plan, it isn't working, there's a new one. Why not?

Ray   I already have.

Pete   What?

Ray   She said it's a good idea too.

Pete (*laughs*)   Just like that. Just like that she said, 'Go ahead, shack up with this bird enjoy yourself.'

Ray   That's right, more or less exactly what she said.

Pete   You actually went to see her?

Ray   Yeh, she had a . . . mole on her lip.

Pete (*sotto voce*)   I don't believe it . . .

Pause.

Ray   It's going to be all right, Pete.

Pete   Come on, Ray, this is stupid. It's stupid!

Ray   Don't worry about it.

Pete   I can't help worrying about it.

Ray   You have a business to run.

Pete   I know, yes I know that –

Ray   And there's nothing you can do anyway.

They look at each other.

Handbag by Mark Ravenhill

Suzanne, thirties; Lorraine, late teens; both any accent.

Suzanne works for a marketing company. In order to find out about the products they advertise, she lives with 'ordinary folk' and video-records as much as possible about their everyday habits around the product, but very much at arm's length, with no intrusion at all, and no 'getting involved'. She is spending a week in Lorraine's council flat. Lorraine's mother has recently died, and the daughter has stayed on illegally in the flat, but she is not coping too well.

Suzanne's partner, Mauretta, is expecting their child any moment now – sperm donated by close friend Tom – and they plan to be a family of two fathers and two mothers. She and Mauretta are a close team, though Suzanne is clearly opportunistic. The characterisation of Lorraine in the scene is ambiguous; the extent to which she is aware of any sexual flirtation can be played on a scale of nil to full on . . .

Suzanne *videos* **Lorraine**, *who is eating.*

Suzanne So what's that, Lorraine?

Lorraine It's a pizza.

Suzanne What type of . . . ?

Lorraine Cheese and tomato pizza.

Suzanne A cheese and tomato pizza.

Lorraine Want some?

Suzanne No thank you.

Lorraine   If you want a bit . . .

Suzanne   No thank you.

Lorraine   Is that 'getting involved'?

Suzanne   . . . That's right.

Lorraine   You're not allowed to do that, are you?

Suzanne   There doesn't seem to be . . . I can't see very much cheese.

Lorraine   You oughtta eat something.

Suzanne   In fact, I can't see any cheese at all.

Lorraine   That's right.

Suzanne   So . . . a cheese and tomato pizza with no cheese. That's a bit unusual.

Lorraine   There was cheese.

Suzanne   Yes?

Lorraine   But I scraped it off.

Suzanne   I see. / Scraped it off.

Lorraine   Yeah. Scraped it off. Go on. Taste it. It's nice.

Suzanne   Why did you scrape it off, Lorraine? Don't you / like the cheese?

Lorraine   You'll waste away, you will.

Suzanne   Why did you buy a cheese and tomato pizza and scrape off the cheese?

Lorraine   Do you think I'm weird?

Suzanne   I'm not here to pass judgement.

Lorraine   You think I'm weird,

Suzanne   No, no, no.

Lorraine   You think it's stupid, scrape off the cheese.

Suzanne   No.

Lorraine   Taste it.

Suzanne   . . . No.

Lorraine   Maybe it is stupid.

Suzanne   Hey, we're all a bit stupid sometimes. Sometimes I'm very stupid. Sometimes I'm totally bonkers.

Lorraine   You're not.

Suzanne   I am.

Lorraine   You're not.

Suzanne   So why did you scrape off the cheese, Lorraine?

Lorraine   My mum used to scrape off the cheese.

Suzanne   I see. Your mum used to scrape off the cheese.

Lorraine   That's right.
Little bit. You know you want it.

Suzanne   Well . . . thank you.

Lorraine   You're involved now.

Suzanne   Not really.

Lorraine   Put it down [*the camcorder*] for a minute.

Suzanne   No.

Lorraine   You're always on the job you, aren't you?

Suzanne   Not always, no. Just now . . . I'm . . . I'm on the job now.
So. Your mum used to scrape off the cheese but now she . . . She used to but now she . . . Lorraine?

Pause.

Lorraine?

Lorraine   She died. Last month, she died.

Suzanne   I'm sorry.

Lorraine   Yeah, well, done now, isn't it?

Long pause.

Suzanne   Lorraine . . . I'm sorry.

Long pause.

Lorraine   There's lots more in the freezer. You can have a whole one.

Suzanne   No. Thank you.

Lorraine   Alright then.

Suzanne *comes over. Hesitates. Hugs* **Lorraine**.

Lorraine   What was that for?

Suzanne   Just because . . . I didn't mean . . .

Lorraine   It's alright . . .

Suzanne   Yes?

Lorraine   Yeah. It was nice.

Pause. **Suzanne** *hugs* **Lorraine**. *Kisses the top of her head.* **Lorraine** *laughs, kisses the top of* **Suzanne**'s *head. Pause.* **Suzanne** *kisses*

Lorraine's *lips lightly,* **Lorraine** *laughs, kisses* **Suzanne**'*s lips.*
Pause. **Suzanne** *kisses* **Lorraine** *on the mouth for some time.*

Lorraine   I didn't mean tongues.

Suzanne   No?

Lorraine   No. I didn't mean that.

Suzanne   Oh.

Suzanne *continues videoing.*

Lorraine   . . . It's not like I ever liked her. Used to lie awake
sometimes. Used to lie awake and think: Wish you'd die. Wish you
were dead, you old witch. But now . . . now . . . I . . . I go down the
shops the same time as her. I watch her programmes. I wear her
clothes. I put on her clothes and I watch her programmes and I eat
pizza like she used to eat pizza.

Suzanne   I see.

Suzanne *puts down the camera.*

Lorraine   You don't have to stop.

Suzanne   I think maybe . . .

Lorraine   I don't want you to stop.
And if the phone goes and it's the double glazing and that I don't
say: 'No. She's dead.' I say 'speaking'. I do her voice and I say
'speaking'.

Suzanne   Listen . . .

Lorraine   I feel so empty.

Suzanne   Listen, Lorraine, let's . . .

Lorraine   Why do I feel . . . ? It's not like I ever liked her.

Suzanne *puts down the camera.*

Honour by Joanna Murray-Smith

Claudia, thirty; Honor, fifties; both any accent.

The play is a sequence of painful scenes that illustrate the breakdown of a thirty-two-year marriage. A renowned poet when she met George, Honor gave up her promising career to bring up their daughter. She has borne no grudges and has believed her life to be truly fulfilled; intellectually like-minded, his success has been as much hers. George is having a piece written about him for a book. The author is a dazzlingly brilliant and beautiful journalist, Claudia. In the course of a few days George and Claudia fall in love, and Honor, who initially befriended Claudia, sees she is losing everything to this younger version of what she might have been.

In this scene, Claudia has agreed to a meeting with Honor, who hopes to talk her out of taking her husband – which is very much how she sees it – explaining that George is going through a midlife crisis.

Honor   What does that mean?

Claudia   What?

Honor   How do you *know*?

Claudia   How do I know? Who can put that into words?

Honor   Well. Well. *I* can.

Claudia   You think you can bully me into explaining myself?

Honor   I want to understand. *How do you know you love him?*

Claudia   I don't have to convince you –

Honor   No. You don't. But I'm asking you.

Claudia (*rising to her challenge*)   When I'm with him, I feel –

Honor   Go on –

Claudia   I feel –

Honor   Say it!

Claudia   All right! All right! I'll say it. I feel as if . . . I'm capable of anything –

Honor   Capable?

Claudia   Yes! Of doing something. Of *being* something.

Honor   You love how George makes you feel!

Claudia   Yes! Yes! All right!

Honor   That's not love!

Claudia   That's love!

Honor   That's child love! You feel *young* –

Claudia   Yes, I feel young! I *am* young.

Honor (*astonished*)   *You think that's love?*

Claudia   And I do the same for him! With me, he wants to *do* things – to do *great* things –

Honor   So you invest him with greatness! My, if you'd come along a little earlier, he could have won a Nobel Prize.

Claudia (*defensive*)   I *facilitate* his greatness. Yes. Yes. I *know* I do.

Honor   The love of reciprocal flattery!

Claudia   Well, at least it's reciprocal!

Honor   What a brutal little thing you are . . .

Claudia   I always considered you very dignified, Honor. Dignity's your thing, isn't it? It's the older woman's singular advantage. You don't want to lose that.

Honor   What are you so frightened of?

Claudia   Nothing. I'm not frightened of anything!

Honor   You're terrified you might lose something . . . What? Certainty? What happened to you?

Claudia   What does that mean?

Honor   What calamity happened to you that you must bring calamity to others? What made you predatory?

Claudia   I don't *need* to be predatory! Your husband has not felt love – real, sexual love for you for years.

Honor   That's not – Not –

Claudia   You said yourself –

Honor   I did *not*!

Claudia   I have it on *tape,* Honor.

Honor   That's right. You taped me! You taped me because I was useful to you.

Claudia   So what if I did?

Honor   You have a genuine talent for pragmatism, don't you, Claudia?

Claudia   What's talent *without* pragmatism? You ought to be an expert on that. When are women like you going to understand that men don't *desire* martyrs? They want women who want things for themselves.

Honor   I suppose you'll be putting George on your C.V.?

Claudia   Well, he's certainly been on yours for long enough.

Beat.

Honor   I never realised – How – How savage you were –

Claudia   I like the truth. The truth is savage.

Honor   You like this, don't you?

Claudia   Like what?

Honor   At first I just thought that you – you were in the – like George – in the grip of something – but you're not, are you?

Claudia   I don't know what you're talking about.

Honor   You really enjoy this, don't you? You like to be at the *centre* of things.

Claudia   *You* asked *me to* come here –

Honor   And you're certainly not going to forfeit your – your *significance,* are you, Claudia?

Claudia   The difference between us, Honor, is that I don't intend giving up *anything* for *anyone.*

Honor   And that makes you feel very proud, doesn't it?

Claudia   Why shouldn't it? (*Beat.*) Look at me. (*Beat.*) Look at all I might become. (*Beat.*) Wouldn't you wish that for yourself? (*Beat.*) You could have been a great writer, Honor. You could have been up there – if you'd been more like me.

Honor   So I should admire you. Is that it?

Claudia   Your husband and I may have fallen in love but – but you and I – are still, on some level, greater allies than – than – he and I.

Honor   *We* are allies?

Claudia   You're a passionate woman – I *know* that. And you have – you're a writer. All around us there are systems to keep us *unrealised*. (*Beat.*) 'Softly, we make a child while from the cliffs, my father's ashes rain down on us, soft as silk.'

Honor   Don't *you* use *my* words.

Claudia   You should never have lost that part of you.

Honor   I still write!

Claudia   You haven't published anything since 1973! All these years, didn't you sometimes wish that all that – that way of feeling and seeing had a place, had a chance? Didn't it wear away at you that lesser talents had their faces in the literary pages while you basted the racks of lamb and looked over George's work? That you never felt the – the warmth of – of being thought great by *others*?

Silence as **Honor** *acknowledges the painful truth of this.*

If anyone can understand me, you should. I'm rectifying your sacrifices.

Honor   You take my husband and you tell me you're on my side?

Claudia   I didn't take him. He offered himself.

Honor   One happy day your face will shift around on those pretty bones and fall from grace.

Claudia   I take care of myself!

Honor   Time takes care of all of us.

Inside Out by Tanika Gupta

Affy, fifteen; Di, seventeen; London accents, but could work in other locations.

This play focuses on the relationship of two half-sisters – one white, one mixed race – who are living with their prostitute mother and her violent and abusive partner/ pimp.

Younger girl Affy's father Tom has made contact with her. Married to another woman at the time of her conception and now widowed, he has offered to give her a home to escape the brutality of the man they refer to as 'Godzilla'. Reluctant to abandon Di, Affy nevertheless eagerly accepts the invitation to move to Brighton, and this sets off a chain of events where Tom reports Godzilla to the police, resulting in his arrest. The girls' mother feels betrayed, as does Di, but for different reasons – she doesn't want to be left behind, and she's tired of not having the apparent privileges that Affy has by being white and having a respectable father, when she is probably the offspring of some unknown punter of her mother's. Despite the tensions, the sisters are very close.

In this scene Di has gone to a riverside location, the place where both girls go to escape when the need arises. Affy has followed her.

It is a glorious day. The sun is shining, **Di** *enters and sits by the river. She looks sullen and angry. She skims stones.*

Affy *enters, sheepishly. She looks guilty. She sits down on the bank quietly.* **Di** *continues to skim stones. They don't say anything for a while.*

Di All packed?

Affy   Yeah.

Di   Great. See ya then.

Affy *looks distressed.*

Affy   You not going to see me off?

Di   No.

Affy   Di . . . please . . . don't be like that . . .

Di   Like what?

Affy *is silent.*

Di   Wanted me to stand in the road waving a white hanky?

Affy *is silent.*

Di   Is that bastard coming to pick you up?

Affy   He ain't a bastard.

Di   Well?

Affy   I'm getting a taxi to the station.

Di   Just fuck off and go, will you?

Beat.

Affy   I'm sorry things didn't turn out the way they should have.

Di   Right.

Affy   You should've been nicer to him.

Di   He's a posh git.

Affy   Why you bein' so nasty? Why can't you be happy for me?
It's what we always wanted. To get out of this place.

Di   Together though, not separately.

Affy   You shouldn't have called him them names.

Di   He shouldn't have wound me up like that.

Affy   He was only trying to give you some advice.

Di   Don't need no arsehole teacher telling me what's what.

Affy *looks upset.*

Di   And as for him goin' to the police about Godzilla.

Affy   He got what he deserved.

Di   And did mum get what she deserved?

Affy   She'll thank me for it one day.

Di   You're beginning to sound like him.

Affy   How can you stick up for Godzilla?

Di   I'm not sticking up for him.

Affy   You and mum, you're just as bad as each other.

Di   Fuck off.

Beat.

Affy *looks at her sister incredulous.*

Di   You broke your word, Affy. I ain't ever gonna forgive you for that. We had a bond.

Affy   What, a vow of silence?

Di   Yeah. You could call it that.

Affy   All I remember is you making plans and me nodding like a fucking idiot.

Di   That's 'cos I'm older, I always looked out for you.

Affy   That don't mean you know best.

Di   Thanks for nothing – bitch.

Beat.

Affy   You want us to say goodbye like this? You could still come down to Brighton, maybe he won't let you live with us but it's a big town . . .

Di   I'll see how things work out.

Affy   What if it doesn't work out?

Di   What d'you mean?

Affy   If you and mum don't get on? If he comes back. You won't stay there if Godzilla comes back, will you?

Di   I'm gonna finish school. Pass me exams this time round. Then I'll make me plans.

Affy   You gotta have a plan now.

Di   Leave it, will ya?

Affy   I'm only thinking about you.

Di   Any plans I make are my business right? I gotta think on my toes now 'cos I ain't got a dad who's gonna suddenly appear out of fucking nowhere, waving a magic wand.

Silence.

Affy   You will come and visit – won't you?

Di   (*relents a little*)   You think that tosser will let me?

Affy   'Course he will.

Di   You could always come and visit us here. Me and mum.

Affy   Yeah.

Di Mum'll calm down soon. 'Specially when she starts missing you. You said goodbye to her?

Affy She won't talk to me.

Di *laughs.*

Affy It ain't funny.

Di She always liked you better and now she's stuck with me.

Affy That ain't true.

Di Never told me stories at bed time to get me to go to sleep.

Di *looks away.*

Beat.

Affy I've gotta go.

Di Go on then.

Affy *stares at her sister.*

Affy We ain't ever been apart, have we?

Di Taxi's probably here by now.

Affy See you then.

Beat.

I'll give you a ring when I get there.

Di Might not be in.

Affy I'll leave a message then.

Di Don't let him boss you around too much.

Affy No.

Di And don't get into no fights at your new school.

Affy No.

Di Look after yourself.

Affy You too.

Di *awkwardly picks up a crumpled-up carrier bag and hands it over to* **Affy**.

Affy What's this?

Di Going-away present.

Affy *looks surprised, she peers in the bag.*

Affy Where d'you get this from?

Di A shop.

Affy *pulls out a very flash-looking camera.*

Affy Must have cost a packet.

Affy *looks at the camera in admiration.*

Di You can't take pictures under water with it but I thought you could do with something to start you off.

Affy Thanks Di. It's . . . it's . . . amazing.

Di There's some film in the bag as well.

Affy *turns the camera over in her hands.*

Affy You nicked it, didn't you?

Di *shrugs and looks away.*

Affy *looks longingly at her sister.* **Di** *does not return her gaze.*

Affy Thanks . . . It's fantastic.

Di You like it then?

Affy 'Course I do.

Di   Bye then.

Affy   Yeah. Bye.

Affy *turns to leave.*

Di *says nothing.*

Affy *exits.* **Di** *waits until her sister has gone. She doesn't cry but looks distraught. She continues angrily chucking stones into the river.*

Little Sweet Thing by Roy Williams

Tash, mid teens, black; Miss Jules, early thirties, black; London accents.

This play investigates what it is to survive the inner-city gang culture that surrounds and informs young people today.

Tash can't afford to drop her tough-girl image. Her beloved older brother, Kev, has just come out of a young offenders' unit and there are guns circulating in her world. She has been fighting fellow schoolmate Donna over a guy, in spite of promising Miss Jules, her schoolteacher, she wouldn't. Having just had her lip cut intervening, Miss Jules has had enough and has finally decided to leave this brutal job and to stop trying to get through to these young people. Nevertheless, she sees a spark of something in Tash, something that is salvageable, some sanity and intelligence, and knows that much of Tash's behaviour is just an act. She has been supportive over the last years, but her resources have now run right down and she wants to prompt some realisation from Tash before letting go.

Tash   Am I as bad as Donna? Go chat to her.

Miss Jules   I can't help her.

Tash   She started the fight. Soon as the head finds out, she'll get excluded.

Miss Jules   What do you care?

Tash   I don't, that's your job. Help her.

Miss Jules   Donna's been warned, she brought it on herself. She's a waste of space.

Tash You can't say that.

Miss Jules I believe I just did.

Tash Call yourself a teacher?

Miss Jules What?

Tash Do you call yourself a teacher? Step.

Miss Jules You know what, you're right. That's the last thing I am.

Tash Believe.

Miss Jules How can I be?

Tash I dunno.

Miss Jules Well, I do.

Tash What you doing?

Miss Jules Packing my things together, then I'm going to get in my car, go home and sleep for a year.

Tash Yes, very funny, Miss.

Miss Jules I'm glad you find it amusing, Natasha.

Tash It was just a fight.

Miss Jules You promised me.

Tash It weren't a real promise. I'm always doing it. You always tell me off for it – that's what we do, Miss. Sit down, man.

Miss Jules 'Is who you barking at?'

Tash Excuse me?

Miss Jules 'Don't tell me what to do, Miss, yeah! Dat ain't happening.'

Tash   Is that supposed to be me?

Miss Jules   'I'm going home to my bed, yu get me?'

Tash   You taking the piss outta me?

Miss Jules   Not nice, is it? I've had enough.

Tash   It was just a fight, you deaf? You said you weren't leaving. You know what, fine, bye!

Miss Jules   Good luck to you, Tash.

Tash   Shit teacher anyhow, didn't learn niche from you.

Miss Jules   What did you say?

Tash   You still here?

Miss Jules   For your information, Natasha, I'm a bloody good teacher.

Tash *grunts.*

Miss Jules   Don't do that.

Tash   I'll do what I like, you're quitting.

Miss Jules   If you opened your ears up more often –

Tash   Oh yeah!

Miss Jules   – you might know.

Tash   Well, come then. Come on.

Miss Jules   Come on what?

Tash   My ears, they're well open now, teach me summin. Show me the goods – come on, Miss, impress me.

Miss Jules   What is this, *Pop Idol*?

Tash   You're such a good teacher.

Miss Jules Tash?

Tash Teach me summin now!

Miss Jules Lose the tone.

Tash You gonna teach me or what?

Miss Jules You are not making any sense.

Tash Teach me.

Miss Jules Natasha?

Tash Teach me.

Miss Jules Are you asking me to stay?

Tash Teach me. Teach me.

Miss Jules Don't make me slap you, yeah!

Tash Wa!

Miss Jules I shouldn't have said that.

Tash Yer bad.

Miss Jules Why can't you answer my question?

Tash (*mumbles*) I did.

Miss Jules What did you say?

Tash Forget it.

Miss Jules Tell me what you said.

Tash No.

Miss Jules This is important.

Tash For who?

Miss Jules Can't you come out of your shell just once?

Tash   Can't you?

Miss Jules   What exactly is it that I am supposed to do? Get down?

Tash *laughs.*

Miss Jules   Hang out with you, be what you want?

Tash   Can you do that?

Miss Jules   Of course not.

Tash   So why you telling me to be what you want?

Miss Jules   I'm the teacher.

Tash   Ex.

Miss Jules   Give me a good reason to stay, then.

Tash   Find your own.

Miss Jules   Look at my face. See how tired I am. You lot with your cheek.

Tash   It's what we do.

Miss Jules   And what I do doesn't matter?

Tash   Course.

Miss Jules   So why don't you listen?

Tash   All I'm doing is messing with you. You do know that? Why can't you just chill, man?

Miss Jules   I'm sorry?

Tash   Let us have our fun, we're leaving soon anyhow, we go join the rest of the spaces out there. All we want is a bit of fun, you have to take that away from us.

Miss Jules   What kind of drivel is that?

Tash   Ain't drivel, yeah, it's true. And you know it as well.

Miss Jules   You think I should stay?

Tash   Up to you.

Miss Jules   What fun exactly? Fighting? Sex up boys?

Tash   I'm not a slag!

Miss Jules   I can't be your friend and your teacher.

Tash   You're giving up.

Miss Jules   So are you.

Tash   Fine then.

Miss Jules   No, Tash, it's not fine. What are we going to do about it? I'm asking you.

Tash   This is just your way of saying we have to do what you want?

Miss Jules   Is that so bad?

Tash   See?

Miss Jules   Trust me.

Tash   You don't understand.

Miss Jules   You're right, I don't understand how you kids live. How you refuse to ask yourselves hard questions about your own lives, what you want from them, your responsibilities. Respect for others, have manners, self-control. No, you're all being force-fed some retarded subculture from the good old US of A.

Tash   You turn Muslim, Miss?

Miss Jules   I am sick of losing another one of you. What is it you want from me?

Tash   You turning it down for a start, you're giving me a headache.

Miss Jules   Listen to me, I will leave.

Tash   Bye.

Miss Jules   You'll never have a teacher like me.

Tash   You love yourself up.

Miss Jules   One who cares.

Tash   Cares?

Miss Jules   Cares!

Tash   Like you care about Donna – a waste of space, you said. You can't teach her, ca you don't know what to do with her. Ca there's nuttin out there for her. Nuttin out there for me.

Miss Jules   No.

Tash   Nuttin out there for Kev, trust you . . .

Miss Jules   Tash, please.

Tash   Don't chat rubbish to me.

Miss Jules   Don't make me leave.

Tash   Stop pretending.

The Memory of Water by Shelagh Stephenson

Mary, thirty-nine; Teresa, early forties; Northern accents, though any accent would work.

In a snowstorm, three sisters are gathering at their late mother's home for her imminent funeral. Eldest daughter Teresa, the deceased's mother's carer, continues to feel put upon and can't hide her disapproval of sister Mary's long-term relationship with Mike, a married man. Mary, an overachieving medical professional, is suffering from hallucinatory dreams in which she speaks to her mother. Having just awoken from one of these disturbing dreams, she doesn't appreciate the intrusion and close questioning she gets from Teresa. To add to the tension, they are awaiting the arrival of youngest sister Catherine, enfant terrible of the family, who is bound to bring problems with her. Mike is also on his way.

This scene comes near the start of the play after a brief dream sequence that hints at something Mary is searching for, which we later find to be information on the son she gave up for adoption after a teenage pregnancy. Mary thinks she's pregnant, but at the same time fears Mike has been lying to her about his relationship with his wife. For her part, Teresa exudes resentment for real or imagined past slights and injustices, while doling out alternative 'medical' advice because sympathy is not her stock-in-trade. Both women think they have the definitive memory of certain events, but who's to say what is real and what is just badly or selevetively remembered? The edginess of both hides fears, but a genuine affection too. The Lucy referred to is Teresa's daughter.

Mary *is lying prostrate. She stirs and gets out of bed, goes to the dressing table, opens drawers, rifles through them. The phone rings.*

Mary   Hello? . . . What time is it? . . . I wouldn't be talking to you if I was, would I? I'd be unconscious . . . Where are you? . . . Jesus . . . you're what? So will you want me to pick you up from the station?

The door opens and **Teresa** *comes in.*

Teresa   Oh . . .

Mary   Hold on . . . (*To* **Teresa**.) It's not for you.

Teresa   Who is it?

Mary (*to caller*)   What? She's gone where? . . . OK, OK. I'll see you later. Are you sure you don't want me to pick you up –

She's cut off.

Hello? . . . Shit.

Teresa   Who was that?

Mary   A nuisance caller. We struck up a rapport.

Teresa   He's not staying here, is he?

Mary   Who?

Teresa   I'm presuming it's your boyfriend.

Mary   How much sleep have I had?

She picks up a portable alarm clock and peers at it.

Teresa   How's his wife?

Mary   Jesus. Two and a half hours.

She flops back on the pillows. Looks at **Teresa**.

Why are you looking so awake?

Teresa I've been up since quarter past five. Presumably he's leaving her at home, then.

Mary You've got that slight edge in your voice. Like a blunt saw.

Teresa I'm just asking –

Mary Of course he's bloody leaving her at home. She's gone to stay with her mother.

Teresa I thought she was ill.

Mary Maybe she went in an iron lung. Maybe she made a miracle recovery. I don't know. I didn't ask.

Teresa Where's he going to sleep?

Mary What?

Teresa You can't sleep with him in that bed.

Mary He's staying in a hotel.

Teresa I thought it might be something important.

Mary What?

Teresa The phone. Funeral directors or something.

Mary We've done all that. Can I go back to sleep?

Teresa And where's Catherine?

Mary She said she might stay over with someone.

Teresa Does she still have friends here?

Mary Probably. I don't know.

She turns away, settles down, and shuts her eyes. **Teresa** *watches her for a while.*

Teresa She could have phoned to say. Anything could have happened to her. It's still snowing.

Mary   She's thirty-three, Teresa.

Teresa   The roads are terrible.

Mary   She'll get a taxi.

Teresa   Probably just as well she didn't come home. She'd have probably drunk four bottles of cider and been brought home in a police car. And then she'd have been sick all over the television.

Mary   She was thirteen when she did that.

Teresa   She was lucky she didn't get electrocuted.

Mary   It wasn't switched on.

Teresa   Yes it was, I was watching it. It was *The High Chaparral*.

Mary   No it wasn't. I wish you'd stop remembering things that didn't actually happen.

Teresa   I was there. You weren't.

Mary *gives up trying to sleep. Sits up.*

Mary   I was there.

Teresa   That was the other time. The time when she ate the cannabis.

Mary   That was me. I ate hash cookies.

Teresa   It was Catherine.

Mary   It was me.

Teresa   I was there.

Mary   So where was I?

Teresa   Doing your homework probably. Dissecting frogs. Skinning live rabbits. Strangling cats. The usual.

Mary   Teresa. I'd like to get another hour's sleep. I'm not in the mood, OK?

She tries to settle down in the bed, and pulls something out that's causing her discomfort: a glass contraption with a rubber bulb at one end. She puts it on the bedside table and settles down again. **Teresa** *picks it up.*

Teresa   Oh, for God's sake . . . Is this what I think it is?

Mary   I don't know. What d'you think it is?

Teresa   A breast pump.

Mary   I found it on top of the wardrobe. I think I'd like to have it.

Teresa   Why?

Mary   Because you've got the watch and the engagement ring.

Teresa   For Lucy. Not for me. For Lucy.

Mary   OK. So you want the breast pump. Have it.

Teresa   I don't want it.

Mary   Good. That's settled. Now let me go to sleep.

Teresa   You can't just take things willy-nilly.

Mary   You did.

Teresa   Oh, I see. I see what this is about.

Mary *sits up.*

Mary   It's not about anything, it's about me trying to get some sleep. For Christ's sake, Teresa, it's too early in the morning for this.

The National Theatre by David Edgar

Eileen, early twenties, London accent, though any other than RP would do; Ella, late twenties, well spoken.

A dressing room backstage at a strip club. Eileen and Ella are fellow dancers and it is about ten minutes before they are about to start the floor show. They are close, and Eileen has recently returned to stripping after a short break following her marriage. She has been very tense and cagey up to this moment, evidently wanting to say something but waiting until they are on their own. Ella is more proficient and less vulnerable than her friend, and has more elevated professional aspirations than taking her clothes off for a living. She trained at RADA, and wants to be a serious actress – she drops into speeches of Masha's from *Three Sisters*, the woman who longs to break away from this provincial hell to get to Moscow, to fulfil her potential. The parallels are obvious.

Eileen Ella.

Ella Yes?

Eileen I got a problem.

Ella Yes?

Eileen 'Bout going on today.

Ella Yes?

Eileen Look at me.

Ella *looks at* **Eileen**.

Ella   Oh, blimey.

Eileen   I put some stuff on, but it's just bringing 'em out.

Ella   You should have said.

Eileen   When?

Ella   Earlier.

Pause. **Eileen** *looks away.*

I see. You couldn't. Not in front of madam. Not expose your tender places to her biting edge.

Eileen (*shrugs*)   OK, forget it.

Ella (*stands*)   Come on, lovely. Let's try a cover-up.

Eileen (*stands*)   They'll come out a treat under the U/V.

Ella   At the moment, they'd come out a treat in the dark. Lie down. Tummy up.

Eileen *lies down, on her back, on the day-bed.* **Ella** *takes a tin of powder, and during the following, tries to cover* **Eileen***'s bruises.*

Eileen   Thanks, Ella.

Ella   You're a right old mess.

Eileen   Yuh, am.

Ella   Can I ask how –

Eileen   Well, I didn't get 'em falling down the stairs.

Ella   No.

Slight pause.

Have you told the police?

Eileen   Well, I can't really. Can I.

Ella   Why not?

Eileen   It's my husband.

Pause.

Ella   Oh. I didn't realise. I thought it was a mugger, or a . . . You know.

Eileen   Yuh.

Ella *still powdering* **Eileen***'s bruises.*

Eileen   You can't, you see, there's no such thing, in legal terms, as your husband raping you. You can't get done, for, as it were, rolling your own.

Pause.

It's funny, 'cos he usually, he doesn't like it much. Gets a bigger rise out of his Alfa, than he does from me.

Ella   Why did he do it, then?

Eileen (*shrugs*)   Punishment.

Ella   For what?

Pause.

Eileen   He knows we need the money.

Slight pause.

Ella   Right. Turn over.

Eileen (*does so*)   I wouldn't mind, but I got this audition.

Ella   What for?

Eileen   Telly. Dancing, with a group of dancers on the telly.

Ella   When?

Eileen   Would you believe, 5pm?

Ella   Today?

Eileen   Today. Don't think he wanted me to get it.

Ella   Why?

Eileen   'Cos his rich chums aren't likely to see me cavorting about here. Or if they do, they're hardly going to mention it.

Slight pause.

Don't you want to? Get another job?

Ella   I s'pose I need to think I do.

Ella *looks away. Pause.* **Eileen** *notices the open sexmag, where it was left, near her, on the floor.*

Eileen   'It wasn't predictable, you understand. He was just standing there, and he said he wanted me. And I laughed, I mean I thought it was a joke, because we'd had this frightful row. Until I saw the bulge in his trousers, and then, without a word, quite suddenly, he hit me, right across the breasts, and shouting, 'Don't you laugh at me, you bitch", he kept on hitting me, I struggled with him, but it wasn't any good, he grabbed my shoulders, roughly forced me down on to the kitchen table,'

Ella *turns to* **Eileen**, *surprised.*

Eileen   'then and there, and held me down with one hand, while he pushed the other up my skirt and started feeling for my bush, beneath my panties, and we both knew at an instant I was wet and really wanted it my slit was pulsing with desire and when he touched my –'

She turns the page of the sexmag. **Ella** *realises* **Eileen** *is reading.*

'Angela. Executive's Girl Friday. Merseyside.'

Ella *takes the magazine.*

Ella   They can't be real.

Eileen   No. Fantasies.

Pause. **Ella** *shuts the magazine. Quite brightly.*

Ella   It may well be, of course, that Sigmund got it wrong. That dirty pictures, masturbation, driving Alfas aren't, in fact, just pale and insufficient substitutes for sex, but that sex is just a pale and insufficient substitute for Alfas, porn and masturbation. Mm?

She opens the magazine again, looks at it.

We all need fantasies. Until the world fills up the gap, between what we have and what we feel we need. Deserve. Our fantasies, cosmetic, so our lives can live with their reflection in the glass.

Pause. She puts the magazine down.

You poor old thing.

Eileen   He said he's going to throw me out. Said, on his own, he wouldn't need the money. Said he didn't need a slut to live off any more.

Ella   Shh. Shh. You poor old thing.

Protection by Fin Kennedy

Grace and Adele, both twenty-four, any accent.

This play offers a behind-the-scenes look at a team of social workers and their clients. Grace is a social-work trainee, working towards a diploma and a permanent position within this team. Adele is an old school friend whose aspirations are much simpler and whose life is more straightforward than Grace's; she is easygoing and pretty thick-skinned, though not uncaring. Grace has been struggling not to upset anyone in her team but at the same time is finding it hard just to toe the line in terms of policy and practice; she has a real sense of responsibility for the clients and is deeply bothered by how the system can treat them. This scene takes place in a bar in Covent Garden where they are having a catch-up drink.

Grace *and* **Adele**. **Adele** *flicking through holiday snaps. She gasps at one in particular and holds it to her chest.*

Adele   God I forgot to tell you! You'll never *guess* who was there on the beach!

Grace   Who?

Adele   Guess.

Grace   I can't.

Adele   Right next to us, perched on a towel. Think school.

Grace   Oh I don't know.

Adele *squints through one eye.*

Grace   What are you doing?

Adele   Think eyeballs. I could've *died*.

Grace   Del, I'm tired.

Adele *holds out the photo.*

Adele   Janet Engelmann.

Grace   Who?

Adele   Glassy! With the *glass eye*. (*Indicating photo*.) There.

Grace   Oh.

Adele   She's still got it right, you can't really see there – but it's a better one now, you'd hardly guess – but she was *there* with *him*.

Adele *holds out another photo.*

Grace   Oh right. Who's that?

Adele   Just the *fittest* model-type diving instructor you've *ever* seen.

Grace   Oh right.

Adele   Apart from he's only got one leg! See?

Grace   Oh yeah.

Adele   It was brilliant! Me and Tony *pissed* ourselves.

Grace   Pretty funny.

Adele   But you know what?

Grace   What?

Adele   She was *really* nice.

Grace   No way.

Adele   Yeah! We got chatting – and get this right – she started her own *prosthetics* company after school. Seriously. Legs and arms and all that. And with all that new money in the NHS and them having to tender out, she's making a *mint.*

Grace   Yeah?

Adele   Yeah! Glassy. Of all people. There in the Azores.

Beat.

Grace   I met a two-year-old girl today. Hospital visit. In for some knock or scrape on her leg. And the doctor's seen these other cuts. Further up. And they go right up. He said they could only have been caused by broken glass.

Pause.

Adele   Oh.

Grace   I'm sorry to put that picture in your head but it's been on my mind.

Pause. **Adele** *puts the photos down.*

Adele   How . . . how do you do it?

Grace   We're prosecuting. He'll get ten years.

Adele   No I mean . . . *you.* How do *you* cope?

Grace   Me? Fuck's sake, Del, I'm the lucky one.

Beat.

Adele   I . . . I admire you.

Grace   Don't be patronising.

Adele   Gracie, I'm not, I'm really not. I just . . . I just don't understand. I can't get my head round why you'd wanna –

Grace   I'll tell you why, Adele. Because no other fucker gives a shit, that's why.

Adele   Hey, calm down, I'm not getting at you.

Grace   And because this stuff – it's going on about two hundred yards in that direction – (**Grace** *points*) – and no-one seems to care. Our lot, us trendy trendy fuckers in here, how many of us give a shit?

Adele   Look what it's doing to you already.

Grace   What?

Adele   Look at you. On edge. You're never like this.

Grace   Why is it 'on edge' to be passionate about my work?

Adele   It's not, I'm not saying that.

Grace   Why is it 'on edge' to care about the people around us?

Adele   You're going off on one, I'm not saying any of that.

Grace   You're in 'media' sales.

Adele   So?

Grace   So what would you care?

Adele   Jesus Christ.

Grace   You and Tony have holidays in The Azores.

Adele   Don't take the moral high ground with me.

Pause.

I couldn't do what you do, that's all.

Pause.

Anyway. She said to say hello.

Grace   Who?

Adele   Glassy. Janet.

Grace   Right.

Pause. **Adele** *offers cigarettes.*

Adele Fag?

Grace No.

Beat.

Yeah. Yeah cheers.

She takes one.

Amadeus by Peter Shaffer

Mozart and Constanze, both twenties, any accent.

Constanze is Mozart's wife. She loves her husband dearly, but is little more than a child who needs looking after. Up to this point in the play we have seen the two of them delighting in each other's company. They are very much in love, but life isn't going too well for them. They have a young son and another is on the way. They are broken as a family. Success, financial and otherwise, has eluded Mozart, not least because his alleged friend, the Court Composer Salieri, has been poisoning his career from the sidelines. Mozart is also physically very ill at this stage.

A crucial figure in Mozart's life was his father, and he measures the deterioration of his life from the point when this beloved parent died. He sees a figure in a grey cloak – a recurring sight – and he believes it to be Death coming to meet him, but Mozart is not ready to die, and is terrified.

Constanze   I'm cold . . . I'm cold all day . . . hardly surprising since we have no firewood.

Mozart   Papa was right. We end exactly as he said. Beggars.

Constanze   It's all his fault.

Mozart   Papa's?

Constanze   He kept you a baby all your life.

Mozart   I don't understand. You always loved Papa.

Constanze   Did I?

Mozart   You adored him. You told me so often.

Slight pause.

Constanze (*flatly*)   I hated him.

Mozart   What?

Constanze   And he hated me.

Mozart   That's absurd. He loved us both very much. You're being extremely silly now.

Constanze   Am I?

Mozart (*airily*)   Yes, you are, little-wife-of-my-heart!

Constanze   Do you remember the fire we had last night, because it was so cold you couldn't even get the ink wet? You said, 'What a blaze' – remember? 'What a blaze! All those old papers going up!' Well, my dear, those old papers were just all your father's letters, that's all – every one he wrote since the day we married.

Mozart   *What?*

Constanze   Every one! All the letters about what a ninny I am – what a bad housekeeper I am! Every one!

Mozart (*crying out*)   Stanzi!

Constanze   *Shit on him! . . . Shit on him!*

Mozart   *You bitch!*

Constanze (*savagely*)   At least it kept us warm! What else will do that? Perhaps we should dance! You love to dance, Wolferl – let's dance! Dance to keep warm! (*Grandly.*) Write me a contredanze, Mozart! It's your job to write dances, isn't it? (*Hysterical, she starts dancing roughly round the room like a demented peasant to the tune of 'Non più andrai!' She sings wildly.*) 'Non più andrai, farfallone amoroso – Notte e giorno d'intorno girando!'

Mozart (*shrieking*)   *Stop it! Stop it!* (*He seizes her.*) Stanzi-marini! Marini-bini! Don't, please. Please, please, please I beg you . . . Look there's a kiss! Where's it coming from? Right out of that corner! There's another one – all wet, all sloppy wet coming straight to *you*! Kiss – kiss – kiss!

She pushes him away. **Constanze** *dances.* **Mozart** *catches her.*

Constanze (*pushing him away*)   Get off!

Pause.

Mozart   I'm frightened, Stanzi. Something awful's happening to me.

Constanze   I can't bear it. I can't bear much more of this.

Mozart   And the figure's like this now – (*beckoning faster*) – 'Here! Come here! Here!' Its face still masked – invisible! It becomes realer and realer to me!

Constanze   Stop it, for God's sake! . . . Stop! . . . It's me who's frightened . . . *Me!* . . . You frighten me . . . If you go on like this I'll leave you. I swear it.

Mozart (*shocked*)   Stanzi!

Constanze   I mean it . . . I do . . . (*She puts her hand to her stomach, as if in pain.*)

Mozart   I'm sorry . . . Oh God, I'm sorry . . . I'm sorry, I'm sorry, I'm sorry! . . . Come here to me, little-wife-of-my-heart! Come . . . Come . . .

He kneels and coaxes her to him. She comes half-reluctantly, half-willingly.

Who am I? . . . Quick: tell me. Hold me and tell who I am.

Constanze   Pussy-wussy.

Mozart   Who else?

Constanze   Miaowy-powy.

Mozart   And you're squeeky-peeky. And Stanzi-manzi. And Bini-gini!

She surrenders.

Constanze   Wolfi-polfi!

Mozart   Poopy-peepee!

They giggle.

Constanze   Now don't be stupid.

Mozart (*insistent: like a child*)   Come on – do it. Do it . . . Let's do it. Poppy!

They play a private game, gradually doing it faster, on their knees.

Constanze   Poppy.

Mozart (*changing it*)   Pappy.

Constanze (*copying*)   Pappy.

Mozart   Pappa.

Constanze   Pappa.

Mozart   Pappa-pappa!

Constanze   Pappa-pappa!

Mozart   Pappa-pappa-pappa-pappa!

Constanze   Pappa-pappa-pappa-pappa!

They rub noses.

Mozart/Constanze (*together*)   Pappa-pappa-pappa-pappa!

Constanze   *Ah! (She suddenly cries out in distress, and clutches her stomach.)*

Mozart   Stanzi! . . . Stanzi, what is it?

Beautiful Thing by Jonathan Harvey

Jamie, fifteen; Sandra, mid thirties; London accents.

Sandra lives with her son Jamie in a block of flats on a south-east London estate. They have a friendly relationship with Ste, who lives next door with his brother and violent father. Ste is sixteen and a frequent visitor, usually escaping from the tyranny of his family. Sandra loves her son dearly but is troubled by reports she has heard of him being bullied at school, his tendency to bunk off and rumours concerning his sexuality. After a worrying call from a teacher, Sandra goes to Jamie's room late at night to try and talk openly with him. Her attitude is not judgemental, but her instincts are to protect her vulnerable child. She is aware that Ste is 'different', and that Jamie looks up to the older, more confident young man. Sandra isn't sure about Ste's sexual orientation, but she suspects he may be homosexually experienced, although this doesn't obstruct her affection for him.

The early hours of the morning; complete darkness. **Jamie** *is in bed.* **Sandra** *comes in, in the dark.*

Sandra   Jamie? You awake? Jamie, I know you are.

Jamie   What?

Sandra   Where've you been please?

Jamie   Nowhere.

Sandra   Oh yeah? It's half-one in the morning actually. (*Pause.*) Where did you go?

Jamie   Out.

Sandra   Jamie! (*She bends and switches on his bedside light.* **Jamie** *doesn't move, lying with his back to her.*) You went the Gloucester, din't ya? Look at me. (**Jamie** *rolls over.*)

Jamie   Only went for a drink.

Sandra   That's where gay people go. They go there and they go Macmillans in Deptford.

Jamie   It's not just gay people who go. Other people go.

Sandra   People like you?

Jamie   Yeah?

Sandra   It's no time for lying, Jamie.

Jamie   It's not a lie.

Sandra   I had a phone call tonight.

Jamie   Oh, you're lucky.

Sandra   From your tutor.

Jamie   Miss Ellis?

Sandra   She's worried about ya.

Jamie   God, coz I bunk off games does it mean I'm gay?

Sandra   No. Coz someone hit you.

Jamie   Everyone gets hit.

Sandra   And called you queer. And it aint the first time. She's worried about what it's doing to ya.

Jamie   I'm all right.

Sandra   Are you, Jamie? Coz I'm not sure you are. I mean, what am I supposed to think? When you're . . . you're going out drinking and coming home at half-one. Getting hit, getting moody, I don't think you are.

Jamie   Well, I am, so go back to bed!

Sandra   Er, I'll go when I'm good and ready if you don't mind.

Jamie   I'm tired.

Sandra   You're pissed.

Jamie   No I'm not.

Sandra   Pissed from a bloody gay bar!

Jamie   How d'you know it's gay anyway?

Sandra   Coz it's got a bloody great big pink neon arse outside of it. Jamie, I'm in the business, I get to know these things!

Jamie   You been spying on me?

Sandra   No. Someone at work seen you go in . . .

Jamie   Don't mean I'm gay . . .

Sandra   Going in with another boy, so who was that?

Jamie (*beat*)   Ste.

Sandra   Ste? Right.

Jamie   Still don't mean I'm gay. They wanna mind their own business.

Sandra   That's what I said.

Jamie   Well then, what you goin' on at me for?

Sandra   Because sometimes, Jamie, I can put two and two together and make bloody four, I'm not stupid, you know.

Jamie   I never said you were!

Sandra   So I think I deserve an explanation.

Jamie   I went for a drink. Big deal. Everyone in my class goes drinking.

Sandra   Yeah, but they don't all go the bloody Gloucester though, do they!

Jamie   Some of 'em take drugs, at least I'm not doing that!

Sandra   I bloody hope you're not!

Jamie   Ah, well, thanks a lot. Thanks a bundle. Go back to bed!

Sandra   I can't sleep, Jamie!

Jamie   Well, don't take it out on me.

Sandra   Jamie. Will you just talk to me?!

Jamie   I'm knackered.

Sandra   Please, Jamie. Talk to me.

Jamie   What about?

Sandra (*sitting on bed*)   I'm your mother.

Pause.

Jamie   Some things are hard to say.

Sandra   I know. I know that, Jamie . . .

Jamie (*crying now*)   I'm not weird if that's what you're thinking!

Sandra   I know you're not, love.

Jamie   You think I'm too young. You think it's just a phase. You think I'm . . . I'm gonna catch AIDS and . . . and everything!

Sandra   You know a lot about me, don't ya? Jesus, you wanna get on that *Mastermind*. Specialised subject – Your Mother. Don't cry. I'm not gonna put you out like an empty bottle in the morning.

Jesus, I thought you knew me well enough to know that. Why couldn't you talk to me, eh? Going behind my back like that, getting up to allsorts. There's me going to bed of a night feeling sorry for ya, coz you had to share a bed with Ste. And . . . and all the time you were . . . you were doing a seventy minus one . . .

Jamie What?

Sandra Think about it.

Jamie *tuts.*

Sandra Do you talk to him?

Jamie Me and him's the same.

Sandra He's sixteen years of age, Jamie. What pearls of wisdom can he throw your way? He aint seen life. He's never even had a holiday.

Jamie It's difficult, innit?

Sandra Am I that much of a monster?

Jamie No!

Sandra Don't get me wrong. I like the lad. Always have. All I'm saying is he's young.

Jamie He's good to me.

Sandra Is he?

Jamie Yeah.

Bedroom Farce by Alan Ayckbourn

Nick and Jan, both anything from mid twenties to late thirties, any accent.

Married couple Nick and Jan have been invited to a house-warming party of close friends. Following a stressful time at work, high-flyer Nick has hurt his back and is now confined to bed. Undeterred, Jan has gone alone, where she has unintentionally met up with her old flame, Trevor. Flattered by his passionate attentions, and frustrated by her emotionally repressed husband's lack of responsiveness, she has allowed Trevor to kiss her. This has been witnessed by his estranged and deeply neurotic wife, Susannah, who has a tantrum and causes the party to be aborted, at which point Jan returns home.

She finds that hypochondriac Nick has fallen out of bed earlier in the evening, been unable to get back in, and is not hiding his resentment at having been abandoned. There is no doubt they love each other, but neither is able to communicate what they want from the other emotionally.

This scene can be recorded lying down or, if you want a challenge, standing up!

Nick *is still lying on the floor.* **Jan** *arrives back.*

Jan   Nick. Nick . . .

Nick   Aaaah.

Jan (*seeing him*)   Darling, what are you doing?

Nick   What do you think I'm doing? I've been lying here for hours.

Jan   Oh, darling. How did you get there?

Nick   I dropped my book.

Jan   (*trying to find a way to get him up*)   Well, let me – how do I get you – shall I . . . ?

Nick   No, no. Don't do that. Let me climb up you.

Jan   Right.

Nick   Can you take the weight?

Jan   Hang on. Right. (*She takes his arms and pulls.*)

Nick   Hup – right – hold steady. Steady . . .

Jan   I'm trying. I'm trying.

Nick   Keep still.

Jan   You are very heavy.

Nick   Right. Nearly there.

Jan   Oh . . .

Nick   What?

Jan   You're on my foot.

Nick   All right.

Jan   Please get off my foot.

Nick   I will. Wait a minute.

Jan   Oh dear God, my foot.

Nick   Right. Hold on, hold on.

Jan *loses her balance. They both crash on to the bed,* **Nick** *falling across* **Jan** *who is trapped underneath him.*

Nick   Aaaaah. Aaaah. Aaaah.

Jan   Aaaah.

Nick   Aaaah.

Jan   Oh, that was agony.

Nick   Aaaaah.

Jan   Can you get off me, darling?

Nick   I cannot move at all. Ever again.

Jan   Well, try to move. I'm trapped.

Nick   I'm sorry. If I could move I would but I'm physically incapable of moving.

Jan   Can you get off my ribs? You're so heavy.

Nick   I am not heavy. I am the correct weight for a man of my height.

Jan   Well, that is still bloody heavy. (*Easing herself slowly underneath him.*) Hang on, I'll try and – oouf. (*She rests.*)

Nick   Did you have a nice evening?

Jan   No,

Nick   Didn't think you would. Serve you right for going.

Jan   Thank you. Here we go again. (*She renews her efforts to slide from under him.*) Huh. Huh – hoo – hup – oh dear God. This is going to take all night. Can't you even roll over?

Nick   Ha ha . . .

Jan   Well, can you be a gentleman and take your weight on your elbows?

Nick   No. That puts a direct strain on all the muscles all the way . . .

Jan   All right. Sorry. Oh dear. (*She laughs.*) We're going to be like this for ever. People will find us in years to come. They'll all jump to the wrong conclusions, failing to realize what a rare occurrence this is. Us together on the bed.

Nick There's no need to get unpleasant.

Jan Sorry.

Nick I've been working very hard lately.

Jan Yes, all right, I'm sorry.

Nick And now thanks to my back, we may have to get someone in for you. Try again.

Jan Humphh – oh – I'm so weak.

Nick You're telling me.

Jan Nick.

Nick Mmm?

Jan While I've got your attention . . .

Nick Mm?

Jan I want to tell you something.

Nick I can hardly avoid listening.

Jan Good. I'm telling you because a I want to tell you and b I've a feeling if I don't a certain person will be phoning you up very shortly to tell you herself.

Nick Who?

Jan Susannah.

Nick Susannah?

Jan Well, very simply – or not very simply – I had a long talk to Trevor.

Nick Ah-ha . . .

Jan   Which culminated in Trevor kissing me.

Nick   I see.

Jan   And to be perfectly honest, with me kissing Trevor.

Nick   Just kissing him?

Jan   Yes. Nothing else.

Nick   Oh, well. Hope you enjoyed it.

Jan   Yes I did, thank you.

Nick   Good. I hope you don't want me to start jumping about with rage.

Jan   No. Not at all. Not at all. (*She slides out from under him.*) Right. Now let's get you into bed. (*Without a lot of ceremony.*) Come on. (*She pushes him up the bed by his knees.*)

Nick   Careful, careful.

Jan   Come on, it doesn't hurt.

Nick   Don't start taking it out on me just because . . .

Jan   I'm not taking it out on anyone.

Nick   As you say, you only kissed him. If you want me to knock you about, you'll have to wait until I'm better.

Jan   I don't want anything, thank you.

Nick   You only kissed him.

Jan   Yes, quite. I went to bed with all the other men at the party but I only kissed Trevor.

Nick   Oh well, that's all right. I had three or four women in while you were out actually. That explains the back.

Jan (*unamused*)   There you are.

Nick   Thank you. Can I have my book, please?

Jan *puts the book on* **Nick***'s stomach, then slams her hand down on the book.*

Jan   There you are.

Nick   Thank you.

Jan   Happy?

Nick   Thank you.

Jan (*pounding the bed rail in fury and frustration*)   Aaarrrggh!

Nick   Did you say something?

Jan   I'm going to wash my hair. (*She picks up a hairdryer from the dressing table.*)

Nick   Wash your hair?

Jan   Yes.

Nick   It's half past twelve.

Jan   So what.

Jan *goes.*

Nick (*mildly amused as she goes out*)   Dear, dear, dear . . .

The Bridge at Cookham by Sheila Goff

Nicky and Teen, both sixteen, both rural Berkshire accents, but any accent would work.

The play is in three scenes, each one a duologue, and each one taking place in the same fifteen minutes of real time; thus during this scene sound effects are heard which are part of the other scenes.

Nicky and Teen are in the same class at school. They are on a bridge spanning the River Thames at Cookham, a picturesque small town in rural Berkshire. In the background, near the bridge, is a pub with a terrace restaurant, the sort that attracts a classy clientele. It's a hot day in summer.

Nicky and Teen fancy each other, but being 'the last virgins in year eleven', taking the next big step in their lives is even more scary than jumping off the bridge into the water, particularly for Teen, and both possibilities warrant some discussion. For Nicky, it's an opportunity to show how fearless he is.

Nicky   Nice up here.

Teen   Have you put any cream on your shoulders?

Nicky   Course not. I want a tan.

Teen   You'll get cancer.

Nicky   Don't talk soft.

Pause.

Teen.

Teen   Give it a rest, Nicky, you're getting boring.

Nicky (*close*) Ah, Teen.

Teen Don't.

Nicky (*close*) You're gorgeous.

Teen Yeah, right.

Nicky (*close*) You are. You've got freckles on your chest. How far do they go?

Teen Don't even think it.

Pause.

Nicky You want me to beg.

Teen Yep.

Nicky So if I beg.

Teen In your dreams.

Nicky God, Teena. I'm going barmy here.

Pause.

You're the last in our year, you know.

Teen I don't think so.

Nicky The last virgin in year eleven.

Teen Oh, I think there's at least one other.

Nicky Even Pig's done it.

Teen So she says.

Nicky So Adam Rees says. He should know.

Teen Whatever.

Nicky Geography field trip. He says she –

Male/Female

Teen   Shut up, Nicky.

Nicky   No, listen.

Teen   Shut up or push off.

Nicky   Don't you want to?

Teen   Want to what?

Nicky   Don't tease.

Teen   Pathetic.

Pause.

Nicky   It's not natural.

In the distance the clock on Cookham church strikes three.

Three o'clock.

Teen   So? You going somewhere?

They kiss, briefly, once.

God, you're so skinny.

Nicky   Wiry, if you please.

Teen   You've got a really nice flat belly.

Nicky   Oi. Tickles.

Teen   It's not fair, I hate you.

Nicky   You're alright. You're womanly.

Teen   Oh thanks.

Nicky   What?

Teen   Shall I get a belly ring?

114

Nicky Oh yeah.
Am I going brown?

Teen You're going red. Oh, Nicky.

Nicky What's that?

Teen You've got little gold hairs on your chest. That is so sweet.

Nicky Hormones.

Teen Hormones!

Nicky It's terrible being a bloke.

Teen I know. Poor Nicky.

Nicky Teen. I really do fancy you.

Teen Do you?

Nicky Yeah.

They kiss again, longer.

Teen Nicky.

Nicky Yeah?

Teen Should I get that top, d'you think?

Nicky What top?

Teen That blue top in Morgan's sale. I showed you.

Nicky Is that what you're thinking about?

Teen Yeah.

Nicky I give up.

Teen What?

Nicky No, I mean it, I give up.

Teen Should I though?

Nicky Don't ask me.

Teen Don't sulk. Where you going? Get down, you plonker, you'll fall in.

Nicky I won't. Come up here, Teen.

Teen No way, you'll kill yourself.

Nicky (*fooling*) Aagh!

Teen Careful!

Nicky Alright, everybody! Look, Teen, look at that lot down there.

Teen Leave it.

Nicky Pretending not to notice.

Teen They're trying to have a quiet lunch, you fool.

Nicky It's the middle of the afternoon. Why aren't they at work?

Teen Behave.

Nicky What you saving it for, anyway?

Teen Sorry?

Nicky What you saving it for?

Teen Oh thank you, Prince Charming.

Nicky It's a question.

Teen What's next, 'If you loved me you would'?

Nicky You would.

Teen The Adam Rees school of seduction I take it.

Nicky It does it for him, yeah.

Teen   Only with Pig.

Nicky   Ah, so she did,/ I thought –

Teen   /I'm saving it, as you so sweetly put it, for a bloke who knows what he's doing.

Nicky   Then I'm your man.

Teen *laughs raucously.*

The Country by Martin Crimp

Richard, forty, British middle class; Rebecca, twenty-five, American.

Richard and Corinne have moved to the country to escape urban life, bringing their children to what should be an idyllic setting. One evening Richard, a doctor, returns home carrying an unconscious woman whom he claims to have found injured at the side of the road. She is Rebecca, a young American woman with a mysterious background.

The following morning she is alone with Richard in the house. This appears to be their first conversation together. Or is it? Suddenly the harmonious natural setting of the countryside takes on a more puzzling unexpected timbre, where language is unsettling and motives impenetrable.

In the play the lines are allocated no names but this scene begins with Richard speaking. An oblique (/) indicates an overlapping line of text.

Richard *enters with a glass of water and gives it to* **Rebecca**. *She sips.*

—So you've not seen Corinne?

—What? Your wife? (*Slight pause.*) I've already told you: I woke up. I was alone. In a strange house. I was afraid. So no: I have not / 'seen Corinne'.

—You haven't heard her move about?

—I've heard no one move about. I've heard nothing. Why would your wife / move about?

—If she was awake. If she was awake, she would move about.

Pause.

She would pace about.

—Can I take a shower? Where is it?

—No.

—Is it through here?

—No. You can't. You can't – I'm sorry – take a shower.

—Do I go through here?

—No, that's . . . that's . . .

What is it?

Pause.

What is it?

—You don't go through there.

—Where do I go?

—You don't. It makes a noise.

—What noise?

—Yes.

—Does it?

—Yes. I'm sorry.

Pause.

—I won't make a noise.

—You *will* make a noise. I'm sorry, but you *will* make a noise.

—What noise? I won't / make a noise.

—The noise it makes. The noise of . . .

—Your shower makes a noise? What / noise?

—The noise of showering.

—Of what?

—Of showering. The noise of / the water.

—Your shower makes a noise of showering?

—Unfortunately, yes.

   Pause.

— You mean the water?

— The water and also the curtain makes a noise on its
   track.

—What kind of noise?

—A kind of screeching, a kind of / screeching noise.

—I won't touch – well in that case I simply won't touch
   the curtain.

—It makes a / noise. No.

—I'll just shower.

—No. I'm terribly sorry. No.

   Pause.

   You'll wake my wife. You'll wake / the children.

—How will I do that? I can't / take a shower?

—*Listen* to me.

—I mean how exactly do you propose to . . . propose to . . .
   enforce . . .

—What?

—Enforce – yes – this prohibition?

—Please, I'm just / asking you.

—With violence?

—I'm just asking you not to use / the shower.

—With violence? Really?

—No. Listen. Let me explain. The shower – not with violence – the shower is up the stairs . . .

—Okay.

—You go up the stairs, but the shower is through –

—Thank you. So I go up the stairs.

—Yes. But no — no, you don't go up the stairs because what I mean is, is you have to pass through their room. The shower is through the children's room. Now do you see?

—It's through your children's room.

—Yes.

—I see. Your children.

—Yes.

—But why is that?

Pause.

Why is your house designed like that? Why do you pass through your children's room to reach / your bathroom?

—It's not a house.

—It's not a house?

—No, it's not a house, it's a . . .

—What is it?

—I'm telling you what it is. You know what it is. You know it's not a house, it's a granary, it's a . . .

—It's a granary.

—It *was* a granary. It was for grain. It was not a house. *Now* it's a house. And of course I'm not – you know I'm not – threatening you. I'm appealing – simply – d'you understand – appealing to your reason.

—But is this reasonable?

—Is what reasonable?

—This . . . route.

—Route.

—This strange – yes – route to your bathroom. Is this a reasonable route?

—I believe so. Yes. In fact it's always been a very good route – an ideal, you could call it, route.

—Until now.

—*Even* now.

—But not for me.

—Not – that's right – for you. Come on.

—What?

—Come on. We're going.

—We're going? Where?

—I'm taking you back.

—I don't trust you to take me back.

—Of course you trust me.

—Why should I trust you?

—I'm taking you back.

—Why should I trust you? You left me.

—I left you, yes, but I didn't *leave* you, and now I'm taking you back. I've *come* back, and I'm *taking* / you back.

—But this is my home.

—This is not – I'm sorry – your home.

—Then why did you bring me here?

—You know why / I brought you here.

—Was it to offer me a position?

—To do what?

—To offer me a position? To help your wife? To be the maid. Was it to be the maid?

—She doesn't need help. She's very capable.

—Get a maid. Fuck the maid.

—I don't want to fuck the maid.

—Everyone wants to fuck the maid.

—Well not me. In fact the opposite.

—The opposite? Really? (*Faint laugh.*)

—Yes really. Is that / funny?

—And what is the opposite of fucking the maid?

—The opposite of fucking the maid is not fucking the maid.

They both laugh quietly.

Dead Funny by Terry Johnson

Eleanor, thirty-nine; Richard, thirty-six; any accent.

This is the opening scene of the play.

Richard is unable to have sexual relations with his wife, Eleanor. They have been together for ten years and she is desperate for a child. So to help them overcome this difficulty, they have been attending counselling with 'Miriam'. Miriam has set them a one-hour exercise to conduct twice a week, where they move, progressively, a little nearer to intimacy. Richard is a consultant obstetrician, like his father before him (which explains the plastic torsos littered about the room); he is also a leading light in the Dead Funny Society – a group of like-minded folk who actively appreciate the comedians of the bygone era, such as Sid James, Benny Hill, Frankie Howerd, Max Miller, by gathering to watch the film footage; each also dresses as his favourite comedian and recites whole routines in character. Eleanor is not a fan.

It is a Wednesday night, and Richard is somewhat distracted from the normal physical arousal routine, by the delightful news that Norman Wisdom is playing at Wimbledon Theatre.

Eleanor *sits, motionless. On the floor, scattered toys and the torso, its organs spilled.* **Richard** *enters.*

Richard   One night only. Wimbledon Theatre. Sunday night. Norman Wisdom. Norman Wisdom.

Eleanor   Lucky Wimbledon.

Richard   One night only.

Eleanor   Might have been a whole week.

Richard   Mr Grimsdale!

Eleanor   You got a ticket?

Richard   I got twelve.

Eleanor   Handy. When you fall asleep you can stretch out.

Richard   Don't laugh at me, 'cos I'm a fool.

Eleanor *laughs, softly and ironically.*

Richard   What are you doing?

Eleanor   Not hoovering up that digestive biscuit.

Richard *finds the torso.*

Richard   Bloody hell, Eleanor.

Eleanor   What?

Richard   This isn't a toy.

Eleanor   It's fun to play with.

Richard   I don't like it being touched.

Eleanor   If you don't want it touched put it somewhere it can't be touched.

Richard   I've had this since my father died.

Richard *finds scattered organs, sits to replace them in torso.*

Eleanor   I know; I live with it. And that.

Richard   Don't start.

Eleanor   Well, isn't it about time they were given a decent burial? Couldn't you help them through the pearly soft hatch and up to attic heaven?

Richard   It's an antique.

Eleanor   No, Richard, a chair is an antique. A porcelain doll is an antique. Some poor Victorian sod's fibula is not an antique. God, they give me the creeps.

Richard   What they give you is an uncomfortable sense of your own mortality.

Eleanor   I'll give you an uncomfortable sense of your own mortality one of these days. I'll give you a permanent bloody sense of your own mortality!

Richard   The heart's missing.

Another ironic laugh from **Eleanor**.

Jesus.

Eleanor   Do you realize how old I am?

Pause.

I'm three years older than you.

Richard   You know I can never . . .

Eleanor   You must.

Richard   Remember.

Eleanor   Everyone knows how old they are.

Richard   I'm . . . thirty-five.

Eleanor   Thirty-six.

Richard   Thirty-six.

Eleanor   Time just passes you by, doesn't it? While the rest of us get dragged along. It's a quarter to nine.

Richard   So what?

126

Eleanor   It is late, Richard.

Richard   Don't call me Richard.

Eleanor   That's your name.

Richard   I know, but I don't like you calling me it. Look, I went to a pub. I had a drink.

Eleanor   Why tonight?

Richard   Why not?

Eleanor   In case you've forgotten, which I don't think you have, it's Wednesday.

She stands, hands him the heart of the torso, then gathers toys.

Richard   I know.

Eleanor   Well then.

Richard   Well then what?

Eleanor   You know what!

Richard   This is broken. Look, he's bloody well broken it.

Eleanor   Then you shouldn't leave it lying around to get broken.

Richard   I didn't leave it lying around; I left it in a perfectly appropriate place.

Eleanor   I hate that word. Appropriate. You never stop using it.

Richard   Because it's often the most appropriate word, presumably.

Eleanor   And that one; presumably.

Richard   If my vocabulary annoys you so much, why do you insist on having these cryptic fucking conversations?

Eleanor   Presumably, Richard, because I think it's appropriate to do so. Richard.

Richard   Don't try to be cleverer than you are.

Eleanor   This is deliberate, isn't it? You're picking a fight.

Richard   I've had a difficult day.

Eleanor   Putting stuff between us. Pushing me away.

Richard   I've just done five hysterectomies. I really don't need this.

Eleanor   What?

Richard   All this.

Eleanor   How were they?

Richard   What?

Eleanor   The hysterectomies.

Richard   What do you mean, how were they?

Eleanor   How were they?

Richard   Uncomplicated.

Eleanor   And the patients?

Richard   Unconscious.

Eleanor   Can you remember their names?

Richard   Whose names?

Eleanor   When you're up to your wrists in someone . . .

Richard   Eleanor . . .

Eleanor   Is she still . . . Jennifer Simpson or is it just offal and chops?

Richard   What's wrong with you?

Eleanor   What were their names? These unconscious women whose uncomplicated wombs you whipped out today. I want their names.

Pause.

You don't know, do you?

Richard   Of course I know.

Eleanor   Go on then; tell me their names.

Richard   Christ, you're in a mood.

Eleanor   I knew you didn't know them.

Richard   I know them.

Eleanor   You don't.

Richard *puts the broken heart in place and closes the torso.*

Eleanor *winds and sets an alarm clock.*

Richard   A drink would be nice.

Eleanor   I know you. You'll let it get later and later.

Richard   I haven't eaten.

Eleanor   That's all right, I haven't cooked. Any more excuses?

Richard   I've got a verruca.

Eleanor   Did you bring a note from home?

Richard   Eleanor.

Eleanor   What?

Richard   I'm not in the mood.

Eleanor   Well, you never will be. Will you? That's the point, isn't it?

Richard   It just doesn't feel right . . .

Eleanor   I know it doesn't feel right. If it felt right we wouldn't have to do this. It's only an hour of your precious life.

Richard   Every other evening.

Eleanor   Twice a week.

Richard   For how long?

Eleanor   That's up to you, isn't it?

Richard   If it was up to me we wouldn't be doing it. If it was up to me I'd be sitting with a meal in front of me watching television.

Eleanor   You're doing this deliberately.

Richard   Doing what?

Eleanor   Making me angry. Making it impossible.

Richard   Eleanor . . .

Eleanor   Why am I Eleanor all of a sudden? I've been Ellie for ten years and all of a sudden I'm Eleanor. I'm only Eleanor when you're being deliberately provocative.

Richard   Don't lose your temper.

Eleanor   And if you tell me not to then you think I will, don't you? Don't you!

Richard   I won't say another word.

Eleanor   Oh, that'll get her, won't it? A bit of martyred silence. That'll make her so bloody angry she'll forget what day it is! Won't she? That'd suit you, wouldn't it?

Richard   Yes, that's right, whatever you say.

Eleanor   Then stay very calm and agree with her and she'll hit the fucking ceiling!! I WILL NOT GET ANGRY WITH YOU, YOU MANIPULATIVE SOD!!!

Richard   Do you want to come on Sunday?

Eleanor   What?

Richard   Norman Wisdom?

Duck by Stella Feehily

Jack, sixties; Cat, late teens; Dublin accents.

Cat is nicknamed Duck because of the size of her feet. She works as a barmaid in a Dublin club belonging to her boyfriend Mark, a loutish businessman and drug dealer. Frustrated by his coldness and lack of consideration, she has torched his new Jeep while out on a night of excessive drinking with a friend. Now she lives in fear of him finding out it was her.

Cat's search for a way to escape the aggression and brutality of life in Dublin underpins the whole play. She likes to appear tough but in reality she's looking for love and tenderness. When Jack, a celebrated writer, comes into the bar and flirts with her, she falls for his charm and sophistication. Flattered by the attention, she goes to his home where they bath together. Note that Cat sits with her back to Jack.

Jack *and* **Cat** *in the bath.*

Cat (*leaning over to kiss him*)   You are very nice when you are sober.

Jack   I've done my best to keep you happy.

Cat   Do my back will you?

He washes her very tenderly.

Jack   You have a magnificent back.

Cat   So you keep saying.

Jack   Well I've seen a lot of it today.

He continues to rub her back.

(*Singing.*) 'You must have been a beautiful baby. You must have been a wonderful child . . .'

Cat   No I wasn't.
I was ugly.
My mouth and eyes were too big for my face.
On seeing me, my dad said 'Can we send her back?'

Jack   He wouldn't say that now.

Cat   Thank god for make-up.

Jack   You are beautiful. You don't need make-up.

Cat   Speaking of which,
You have an interesting array of cosmetics in your cabinet.

Jack   Do I?

Cat   So either you double job as a drag act or someone else lives here.

Pause.

Jack   I have a girlfriend.

Cat   Don't worry it's not infectious.

Jack   You have a boyfriend.

Cat   Where is she?

Jack   She's visiting family in France. She's French. Are you jealous?

Cat (*she is*)   Course not. I barely know you.

Jack   You know me well enough to share my bath water.

Cat   I'm just hoping she?

Jack   Suzanne.

Cat   Is not going to walk in on us.

Pause.

Jack   She's away for a couple of weeks.

Cat   That's convenient.

Pause.

So do you do this often?

Jack   What?
Fall in love with waitresses?

Cat   See other people.

Pause.

Jack   Me and Susie are together a long time.

Cat   How long is long?

Jack   I don't know. About sixteen years maybe?

Cat   You say sixteen years and it's probably twenty-five.

Jack   I stopped counting at ten.

Cat   That's hardly a girlfriend. That's a wife.

Jack   Had one of those too.

Cat   And where is she? The Wife?

Jack   She left me for a Laertes she met on a touring production of *Hamlet.*
Married with children now.

Cat   Is this what you people do?

Jack   What do you mean 'You people'?

Cat   Are you bored? Is that it?
With Suzanne?

Jack   No.
But I suppose . . .
We are more like brother and sister now.

Cat   Oh God.
I've been reading the problem pages for years.
That's what they all say.

Jack   Maybe because it becomes true.
And how long have you been with – ?

Cat   Mark.
One year.

Jack   Not very long.
Do you love him?

Cat   Would I be here?

Jack   In my experience. Yes. It's possible.

Cat (*moving to stand*)   I'm getting out.

Jack (*he holds on to her*)   Do you always run off when you don't like the sound of something?

Cat   Don't think you're anything special to me.

Jack   I think I am.
Turn around.

Cat   No.

Jack   Come on.

Cat   Get off.

Jack   Don't get like this. I love you.

Cat   Stop saying that. It's really boring me.

Jack   You don't mean that.
Are you like this with Mark as well?

Cat   Fuck off.

Jack   God this is like having a cat in the water.
You love me I know you do.

Cat   I think you'll find you're wrong.
I don't know you and you don't know me.

Jack (*he turns her around*)   Kiss me.

They kiss.

Cat   Are you going to look after me?

The Employee by Sebastian Baczkiewicz

Iain and Janey, both early forties, any accent.

Set today or sometime in the future, Iain is in mess. He has just been 'let go' from an organisation he has given his life to. Chief Maintenance Officer for the Elm, a prestigious building designed with a highly sensitive self-maintaining eco system, he was sacked primarily for upsetting too many people. Protecting the building's best interest, he blamed the workers for not caring for the delicate infrastructure of the Elm when there were technical problems. Betrayed to management by a close workmate, he has now just learned that his ex-wife, Janey, has decided to go to Australia with her new husband Ralph, and with Iain's twelve-year-old daughter, Carolyn. Even though they are now separated and she has a new life of her own, Iain still has the ability to drain and exasperate Janey. Jobless, friendless and single, he is desperate and losing his grip on reality, even imagining fantastical sequences, like the karaoke singalong when he was talking to his workmate in the previous scene, and the dropping into Japanese in this; though only he – and the audience of course – seem to hear these sequences.

The yard behind a Japanese restaurant.

Raucous applause and laughter from a Japanese game show which mixes down to street sounds and Japanese TV from an upstairs window. Sirens in the distance. A helicopter passes perhaps.

Iain   Australia?

Janey   You just need to get your head around it.

Iain   Australia?

Janey   We only just had it confirmed.

Iain   Australia?

Janey   You can stop saying it now, Iain.

Iain   When was this decided?

Janey   Nobody decided.

Iain   Somebody decided something, Janey.

Janey   Ralph's company decided.

Iain   And Carolyn?

Janey   Carolyn's coming with us of course.

Iain   This is my daughter we're talking about here.

Janey   Our daughter. And I've been trying to reach you for days.

Iain   There have been work things. Problems.

Janey   When are there not?

Iain   Listen, I can't go into all of this right now.

Janey   We have to have this conversation, Iain. Like it or not. We do.

Iain   Carolyn could live with me.

Janey   Don't be ridiculous. Look, can we go into your flat, Iain, and finish this there?

Iain   Why couldn't she?

Janey   I'm not going to argue about this out here in a yard. And what's that smell?

Iain   The dustmen are late for the fish this week.

Janey And you think a one-room flat above a Japanese restaurant that you won't even let me see is the best place to bring up our daughter?

Iain Better that than flying her off to the other side of the world.

Janey You never see her anyway.

Iain I do my best.

Janey Not if it interferes with work.

Iain I have responsibilities. That's something you clearly have no understanding of.

Janey Nothing changes with you, does it?

Iain Here we go.

Janey The Elm this. The Elm that.

Iain The Elm kept us.

Janey The Elm kept you.

Iain Carolyn didn't leave me. You did.

Janey You were never there. And how dare you talk to me about responsibilities? (*Beat.*) She's coming out with me and Ralph and there's an end to it.

Iain Ralph. How did you end up marrying someone called Ralph Harris?

Janey In much the same way I ended up marrying someone called Iain – two Is in the Iain – Adam. At least Ralph's there for her.

Iain And I'm not?

Janey No, Iain, you're not – and you never were.

[**Makoto** (*from window above*) Hey, you two! Keep it down, yeh, we're trying to watch TV up here.

Iain   Sorry, Makoto.

Makoto   And we need to talk about the rent, Iain.

Iain   I'll come up this evening.

Makoto   About nine?

Iain   Nine works for me.

Makoto *closes the window.*]

Janey (*quieter, trying again*)   Carolyn needs a new start, Iain. She wants this.

Iain   She's twelve years old – she can't possibly know what she wants.

Janey   I'm worried she's messing up.

Iain   Messing up where?

Janey   At school. Everywhere. There are boys.

Iain   What kind of boys?

Janey   The wrong kind.

Iain   She hasn't . . .

Janey   I don't think so. I hope not.

Iain   You don't know? She's twelve years old.

Janey   Try telling her that.

Iain   I want to talk to Ralph.

Janey   I'll get him to call you.

Iain   I know you're doing this to hurt me.

Janey   I think the hurting's all been done, don't you?

Iain   Nothing's more important to me than Carolyn.

140

Janey   If you say so, Iain.

Iain   I want to spend some time with her before you go.

Janey (*in Japanese*)   *Kono koto-wa ato de mata hanashi-mashou.* [We'll speak in the next few days and try and sort something out.]

Iain   What?

Janey (*in Japanese*)   *Mou jyubun yo, mou hanashitaku-waiwa.* [Let's not make this any more difficult than it already is.]

Iain   Why are you speaking like this?

Janey (*in Japanese*)   *Nani yo? Watashi ga nani o itteru te.* [Speaking like what?]

Adam   You're talking Japanese.

Janey (*in English*) I'm what?

Iain   You were talking Japanese.

Janey   I don't know any Japanese.

Iain   Just now.

Janey   What is wrong with you?

Iain   You were talking Japanese.

Janey   You know something, Iain. That building killed you.

She walks away.

File it Under Fiction by Sheila Goff

Jasmine, fifteen; Ken, twenty-three; any accent.

Taken from a set of interconnecting plays inspired by lonely-hearts ads, this is the first scene that introduces Ken and Jasmine. The scene is called 'Good Sense of Humour'; both characters need one, as their relationship is not as straightforward as might appear. Later, she goes on to rob him and it is hinted that there is something more sinister about why 'sir' left the school so suddenly. The extract provides concrete details about both characters while being rich in allusion and suggestion.

   (Close) refers to the microphone position and / indicates an overlapping line of text.

A fairground.

Ken (*close*)   It was a bet.

Jasmine (*close*)   Saw him looking.

Ken (*close*)   A dare.

Jasmine (*close*)   I could see him thinking, do I –

Ken (*close*)   It was Rob's birthday –

Jasmine (*close*)   do I –

Ken (*close*)   or something. I don't know. We were having a drink, half a dozen of us from the office, standing in the sunshine, jackets off. Beer spilt on the slatted table. The noise of the fairground.

Jasmine (*close*)   do I know her?

Ken (*close*)   She looked familiar. She was concentrated on her phone, texting, texting. One hip jutting. Hundreds of girls like that. I steer clear of them. They unnerve me. Their knowing eyes. Their sharp little mouths.

Jasmine (*close*)   And he did know me. Of course he did.

Ken (*close*)   Somebody's idea of a good joke, to get me to go over. To talk to her.
Excuse me, I said. The lads –

Jasmine (*close*)   Behind him, the lads, all weyhey and get in there.

Ken   The lads were wondering –

Jasmine   Hullo, sir.

Ken   Jasmine?

Jasmine   Don't say you didn't recognise me.
(*Close.*) He'd put on weight. But he always was going to be a fat lad.

Ken   Jasmine. How are you? You still at school?

Jasmine   Course I am. Exams this year, remember.

Ken   I forgot. It seems so long ago. And you're so /grown-up.

Jasmine   /Grown-up. You said.
(*Close.*)   He left suddenly. Over the holidays. Something to do with –
Which school you teaching at now?

Ken   I'm not teaching any more.

Jasmine   Shame.
(*Close.*) Something to do with some woman. Her old man came up the school.
You were the best teacher.

Ken   No.

Jasmine   Yes you was. We all liked you. You were a laugh.

Ken   How are the others?

Jasmine   Those your mates? Noisy lot.

Ken   They bet me I wouldn't speak to you.

Jasmine   So this is a bet. Very nice.

Ken   They thought I wouldn't have the bottle.

Jasmine   I hope there's good money in it.

Ken   Just a drink.

Jasmine   Just a drink. Put your arm round me.

Ken   You sure?

Jasmine   Go on, sir. For a laugh.

Encouraging male laughter is heard.

Ken   You'd better call me Ken.

Jasmine   Wouldn't that be insolence?

Ken   I'm not your teacher now.

Jasmine   That's right. Fancy a go on something? A ride.

Ken   I'm not too keen.

Jasmine   If I'm going to earn you a drink, I reckon you owe me that. Leave your arm.

Ken   I'm with the lads.

Jasmine   Not now you're not.

Gulp by Roger Williams

Susie and Luke, both twenties, both from Cardiff, though any accent would work.

Susie likes men: straight ones for fun, gay ones for friendship. She has lived with Rob since his one great love let him down, and has kept his spirits up while he recovered slowly from the loss. Now, though, he's got a new boyfriend, Mark, who has moved in to the flat and is monopolising Rob, who seems to have forgotten she exists. So much for friendship. Susie has pulled tonight and sits with Luke in his car outside her flat, unable to face taking him upstairs to the love nest where she feels like an intruding gooseberry.

The scene starts with some challenging business – acting wild passion within the confines of an imaginary car – and depends thereafter on the interplay between the two characters' different agenda. Luke, aroused, wants to get indoors as soon as possible, but for Susie this usually pleasurable activity has only reminded her of how angry she feels about being alienated in her own home, so she puts the brakes on as she turns from libidinous to livid. At the same time, Luke's frustration gives way to fascinated curiosity.

Luke   Fucking hell.

Susie   Yeah.

Luke   Wow.

Susie   Yeah.

Luke   Jesus.

Susie   Yeah.

Luke Fuck.

Susie Yeah. (*Beat.*) Wanna do it again?

Luke Yeah.

They kiss excitedly. **Luke** *tries to slide his hand into* **Susie***'s dress.* **Susie** *pulls away.*

Susie Oi! Not here. I'm not getting them out for you here.

Luke Why not?

Susie We're in the middle of the bloody street that's why not.

Luke Nobody minds.

Susie Well, I do, and I'm not getting my kit off in a parked car in the middle of the street. Not tonight anyway. I haven't had that much to drink.

Luke No one's looking.

Susie How do you know?

Luke No one's around.

Susie Not now, no. But someone might pop along halfway through and catch us in full flow.

Luke I'm not shy.

Susie I didn't say you were.

Luke *sits back and looks out.*

Luke Can't we go inside?

Susie You're not slow in putting yourself forward, are you?

Luke I've always been keen. Well?

Susie Maybe.

Luke Maybe?

Susie Yeah, maybe, later on. If you behave. There's no rush. You haven't got a curfew, have you?

Luke No, but I think it's a bit stupid us sitting round in a cold car in the middle of the night when there's a nice warm flat lying empty up there.

Susie It's not empty. My flatmate's in.

Luke Is she funny about you bringing blokes home then?

Susie No.

Luke Bit up tight, is she?

Susie Far from it.

Luke Is she the jealous sort then?

Susie Can be. But not at the moment, he's seeing somebody himself.

Luke You share with a bloke? (*Beat.*) So he's like a friend then?

Susie Come again?

Luke Well, are you friends or are you like, y'know, special friends?

Susie God no.

Luke Gormless is he?

Susie No. Rob is just my friend. That's all. Nothing else. We've never shared any bodily fluids whatsoever, just a toilet seat.

Luke So he's up there now then?

Susie Yep.

Luke With his woman?

Susie Sort of.

Luke   Sort of?

Susie   He's up there with his boyfriend.

Luke   Oh God, right, I'm with you now. He's gay.

Susie   Yes.

Luke   And he's up there with his bloke? On the job like?

Susie   Probably.

Luke   So why don't you want to go upstairs then? Don't want to disturb them, is it?

Susie   He's got his own room.

Luke   So what's the problem?

Susie   I just want to stay here for a bit. Admire the view. If that's ok with you?

Pause. **Luke** *looks out the window bemused.*

Luke   So, you don't mind it then? You're not trying to stay out of their way because you don't like it? Them? At it?

Susie   No. They can bonk away till the end of the millennium for all I care. I'll even cheer them on. I just don't want to go in right now. I want to sit here. With you.

Luke   Fine. You're the boss. D'you want the radio on?

Susie   Nah.

Pause.

Luke   The blower?

Susie   Thanks, but I'm right.

Pause. He produces a tin of travel sweets.

Luke   Butterscotch?

Susie Look I'm fine, I don't want anything. So can we just sit here for a minute please? Quietly? There's nothing suspicious about it. I just want to sit here, in your nice new Metro for five minutes before going back into that flat and getting you to give me the screw of the century on the bedroom carpet. All right? Ok?

Luke Fine.

Susie Thank you.

Pause.

Luke (*timidly*)   It's a Peugeot though. Not a Metro. I'd never buy a Metro. My Dad had one but the suspension went and . . .

How Guillaume Apollinaire Saved my Marriage
by Michael Butt

Penny and Bill, both early fifties (but a couple of any age would work), both middle-class English accents.

Penny and Bill have been married for some time. Penny has become aware – due to his lack of subtlety – that Bill has frequent affairs, using an interest in stamp collecting to cover his absences. Confident that she'll never actually lose him, Penny plays along, mildly tolerating his infidelity, but not necessarily lacking the determination to curtail his amorous activities by some clever means.

This extract's use of background telephone conversations and direct comments to the audience make it a good technical exercise for radio acting.

Penny   My husband's a philatelist. And a philanderer. I'll explain.

Bill (*dialling, on phone*)   Hello? Chi Chi? Is that you? I bet you are. What? Chi Chi, of course, you're special. They broke the mould when they . . . What? And not only the mould. They burnt down the factory. What do you think of that? Of course I'm sincere. Listen, why don't we meet? Mmm? To do what? Chi Chi, you are disgusting. Is that physically possible? I'll take your word for it.

Penny   Through half-opened doors and drawn curtains and . . .

Bill (*on phone*)   Marie? Is that you . . . ?

Penny   . . . windows somehow not quite shut I have been subjected to the outpourings of my husband's . . . what shall I call it? . . . hobby. I know what you're thinking.

Bill (*on phone*)   Bridget, you sound very tired. What have you been up to, you naughty girl?

Penny   'Why do I put up with it? Why haven't I thrown him out?'

Bill   Listen, you wouldn't be free this evening, would you, by any chance? (*Then under* **Penny***'s following speech.*) . . . Mmm? Say . . . Sachell's at eight? Say . . . the corner table?

Penny   You see . . . I never wanted to . . . what's the word? . . . confront him . . . it wasn't my style . . .

Bill (*on phone*)   I'll be the gent with the pink carnation.

Penny   . . . I mean, I'm English.

Bill (*on phone*)   You minx!

Penny   . . . and then there was always the philately. His other hobby, which somehow confused the issue. For one thing, it provided him with a suitable excuse for going out and so then I began to think, if I could only deal with that, with the stamp collecting I mean, then the other . . . the philandering . . . would also be taken care of. (*Pause.*) It's funny what your mind tells you, isn't it?

Bill   Got to go out.

Penny   Oh yes?

Bill   Stamp auction.

Penny   Ah. Sort of philatelists' jamboree, sort of thing, is it?

Bill   Not exactly.

Penny   No, but in that area.

Bill   Yes . . .

Penny   You know when you'll be back?

Bill Well, these auctions . . .

Penny Mmm. They go on and on, don't they?

Bill They do.

Penny So what are we saying?

Bill Well . . .

Penny Eight o'clock?

Bill It could be a bit later.

Penny Later?

Bill Than that.

Pause.

Penny How much later, Bill?

Bill It's difficult to put my finger on it exactly.

Penny Is it?

Bill I wouldn't want to deceive you.

Penny Have a shot at it.

Bill Hand on my heart?

Penny Yes?

Bill It could go on a bit later than eight o'clock.

Pause.

Penny And what are you hoping to pick up?

Bill Pardon?

Penny What are you hoping to get your hands on?

Pause.

Bill Well . . . it all de –

Penny Got your eye on something?

Bill A stamp.

Penny Any particular . . . ?

Bill As a matter of fact . . . shall I tell you what I'm really after?

Penny Yes, what?

Bill A one-franc red. 1849. Head of Napoleon III. Very valuable.

Penny Because . . . ?

Bill It's a fake.

Penny Ah.

Bill Which oddly enough makes it worth more than if it was genuine. That's philately for you.

Penny Funny game.

Bill Now that I wouldn't mind getting my hands on. Got to run.

Penny Good luck!

Bill *goes out.*

Penny You see? It wasn't easy. The moment never arrived when I felt . . . able . . . comfortable about actually . . . charging him with . . . I mean . . . but I don't want you to think I did nothing.

Man with a Travel Hairdryer by Katie Hims

Dean, thirty-two; Sandra, twenties; any accent.

Dean is a police officer who has shot and killed a man in the line of duty. The victim, Bodie, appeared to be carrying a gun and was a suspect in an earlier incident. Called out as a member of an armed response team, Dean took the initiative in good faith, followed procedure and opened fire. Later, it turns out that the 'gun' was really a travel hairdryer in a carrier bag which Bodie was collecting from the mender's.

While awaiting a hearing to determine whether he acted legally, Dean, consumed by guilt, decides to go to the hairdresser's salon where Sandra, the dead man's fiancée, works. He hopes to catch a glimpse of her without her knowing who he is and to reassure himself that she is coping, and subconsciously he wants to punish himself for what he's done, albeit accidentally. The sense of isolation brought about by his suspension is made worse by the realisation that his wife can't possibly understand what he's going through.

When Dean comes into the salon Sandra is instantly attracted to him, unaware of who he is. Since Bodie's death she has been in shock, blaming herself for inadvertently causing him to be in the wrong place at the wrong time. Here, her numbed senses are reawakened.

Dean (*voice-over*)   Her name's Sandra. She's a hairdresser. It isn't difficult to find out where she works. Which hairdresser's she works in. And I just want to go and see her. I just want to go and look at her. It's about five thirty when I get there and she's sweeping up. And I am so relieved to see that her face is perfectly normal. And I realise that I expected some kind of a monster. Some kind of horrorfilm face. Because of all the hate. All the hate she must feel for me. But when I look through the window she sees me looking and then what choice do I have? What choice do I have but to go in?

Interior acoustic. Hairdresser's.

Dean Hiya.

Sandra Hi.

Dean Erm.

Sandra Did you want to make an appointment?

Dean An appointment? Well, erm.

Sandra Oh, did you want – do you want a haircut right now?

Dean Is that? Is that possible?

Sandra Yeh. Yeh, I was just going to close up actually but it's fine.

Dean Oh, well, if you were going to. I don't want. I mean, I'll just come back another day.

Sandra It's no trouble. Honestly. Another half-hour doesn't make much difference.

Dean (*voice-over*) She washes my hair and it's a very weird moment. Like this woman has got her hands on my head and she's being really gentle and she asks me –

Sandra Is the water too hot?

Dean No, it's fine.

Dean (*voice-over*) And I wonder if she ever cut his hair. I think she must have done, mustn't she? I mean, if your fiancée is a hairdresser you don't go out and pay someone else. So she must have washed his head many times. She must have dried it like she's drying mine. And this is how it must have felt. And I think how would she react if I told her. If I said who I was right here right now. But I just study her in the mirror. Specially her hair which doesn't look real.

Sandra   It's a wig.

Dean   What?

Sandra   My hair. It's a wig.

Dean   Sorry, I didn't mean to stare.

Sandra   Don't worry about it. People give me that look all the time, trying to work it out, is it, isn't it.

Dean   Well, er, it's a very nice wig.

Sandra   Thanks.

Dean *coughs.*

Sandra   I haven't got cancer or anything. I mean, if that's what you're thinking. Erm, no, all it is is that my hair fell out.

Dean   It just fell out?

Sandra   Yeh.

Dean   Just overnight?

Sandra   No, it took about two weeks. Stress, I think. A lot of people thought I had cancer. So they were relieved when I said, no, it's just me losing my hair. That's not so bad then, people said. I've got five wigs now. Strawberry blonde. Ash blonde. Platinum blonde. Auburn and Raven Black. I'm like a dentist with no teeth. Or a heart doctor with no heart. Sorry, I'm talking too much, aren't I?

Dean   No, not at all.

Sandra   You've got great hair. You'll have your hair 'til you're eighty. No threat of it receding.

Dean   Really?

Sandra   None at all.

Dean (*voice-over*)   But this makes me feel bad. That I will always have my hair. I will always have a full head of hair and she will always be bald and it doesn't seem right. And when I get home I take a long look in the mirror. I examine my hairline and I see that Sandra's right so then I shave my head. When my wife comes in from work she says what have you done to yourself. She says that I look frightening. And it's true. I look kind of scary and if I saw myself in the street I would probably stop myself. I would probably stop myself and say can you get out of the car please. And I'd find nothing on myself and I would have to let myself get on my way but I'd have an uneasy feeling. I would feel uneasy about letting myself go.

The Mortal Ash by Richard Cameron

Rainy, twenty-one; Chris, twenty-three; any regional/rural accent.

Rainy and Chris are sister and brother. Their father, Tom, and brother, Eric, carried out some work for a local contractor, Hicks, filling in a nearby site. The locals had wanted it to be left as it was – a natural playing space.

Following the tragic accidental death of a girl who was playing unnoticed in an area of the site prohibited to the public, the family has been ostracised by the local community. Eric is in prison for physically retaliating during a recent attack, while Tom has not been able to work locally. Chris and his girlfriend, Linda, have moved into a flat they can ill afford; he has barely been back to the family home. Chris and his father had been close but they are now estranged – the blame for the family falling apart hanging in the air between them.

The family are forced together this weekend to celebrate the seventeenth birthday of Duane, the youngest of the siblings.

Rainy   So how are you, then?

Chris   All right.

Rainy   What you been up to?

Chris   Keeping busy.

Rainy   Work?

Chris   While it lasts. How's your place?

Rainy   Crap. 'S a job, though, innit?

Chris Would you work at Asda?

Rainy I might. Work's work. (*Pause.*) Mam told you about things?

Chris I'm fixing the window. (*Pause.*) Were you in when the brick came through?

Rainy Watching telly. (*Pause.*) I saw Linda this morning.

Chris In town?

Rainy She were with her mother in Top Shop.

Chris Did you speak?

Rainy No, they were looking at tops.

Chris You should have.

Rainy Yea, well . . .

Chris She's all right, her mam. (*Pause.*) She is. I know you think she hates us, but she dunt. You're not gunna find out if you keep avoiding 'em, are you?

Rainy No.

Chris Well, then.

Rainy I know. I know.

Chris Linda's all right with you, in't she?

Rainy Yea. I were talking to her 'other week on 'market.

Chris She said.

Rainy Did she get them net curtains she were after?

Chris Yea.

Rainy I bet it looks nice now. Sounds like it was a right dump you moved in to.

Chris   It was.

Rainy   I'm still waiting for me invite.

Chris *looks a bit sheepish.*

Chris   You'll have a long wait.

Rainy   Why?

Chris   Don't say owt.

Rainy   What?

Chris   We're not there any more.

Rainy   Why? What's happened?

Chris   Don't say owt to mam for Christ's sake. I'll never hear the last of it.

Rainy   I won't.

Chris   I couldn't afford 'rent any more after they put me back on basic. Wi'out overtime I'm getting bugger all.

Rainy   So where are you?

Chris   Her mam's for 'time being.

Rainy   After all you've done to it.

Chris   I know. Put a few quid in the place.

Rainy   Put a few hours and all. Painting and what have you.

Chris   Yea, well, if I ant got rent, I ant got it. Her mam's all right about us being there.

Rainy   You'll have to say summat. If mam finds out from somebody else . . .

Chris   Yea, I know. Gunna cheer her up, in't it, me being round there.

Rainy Can't be helped.

Chris Can't come back here, can I?

Rainy It's up to you.

Chris Can you see it working? I can't.

Rainy Maybe you should have taken that cottage when it were offered.

Chris No way.

Rainy I know, but . . . rent free an' all.

Chris I don't want no favours from Hicks. Done enough for us. Set it all up, walks away clean as a whistle and we get all this.

Rainy We? Where were you?

Chris You know what I mean. Shit doesn't stick to money.

Rainy Yea well when you've got none, beggars can't be choosers.

Chris I'd live in a cardboard box before I'd go cap in 'and to that bastard.

Rainy I'll get you one from work.

Chris We'll sort summat out. I'm gunna be looking round for another job anyway. They've already laid off a load. I might be next.

Nabokov's Gloves by Peter Moffat

Nick and Fran, both mid to late thirties, any accent.

Nick, a successful barrister and devotee of football and pop trivia, is emotionally estranged from his GP wife. The title refers to the fact, mentally stored by Nick, that Nabokov, the Russian-born novelist most famous for *Lolita*, the story of an older man's love for a young girl, was a goalkeeper, and that at the time he wouldn't have worn gloves. A lesser-known fact about Nick is that he is recklessly embroiled with a young female client – a small-time drug dealer, Mary Duggan. Darling Campbell-Browne, a work colleague of Nick's, lives in Sussex, near to Mary. Nick has invited himself to her home with some other workmates, including Martin, Darling's married lover, in order to steal a meeting with Mary sometime over the weekend. Nick, though, has been rather slow about telling Fran of this weekend in the country. Fran wants her marriage to work again, though she is tired of reaching out to her husband.

Nick *and* **Fran**'s *bathroom.*

Fran   You've been home for two hours.

Nick   Yes.

Fran   And it takes you two hours to mention this . . . plan.

Nick   What do you mean?

Fran   It's Thursday night. Darling Campbell-Browne has asked – us? – to go down to Sussex for the weekend. Simple question. Why did you wait two hours before mentioning it? Tell me about the process.

Nick This is ridiculous.

Fran Do you want me to come?

Nick Of course.

Fran Your voice goes up an octave.

Nick What?

Fran When you . . .

Nick When I . . . Go on. When I . . . What?

Fran Do you want me to come?

Nick I want you to come.

Fran And then with superhuman effort you bring it back down again and do the best you can with your eyes.

Nick Fran.

Fran Steady gaze, Nick. Very good. But I've seen your eyes look at me . . . I've seen how they *can* look at me . . . remember? Do actually try to remember.

Nick When you're in this kind of mood . . .

Fran Don't.

Nick It's . . . terrible.

Fran It's not my mood.

Nick Yes, it is.

Fran It is not my mood. It's your mood. That's the whole point. Why can't you just be honest. You don't want me to come to Darling's. Do you? Why?

Nick I didn't say I didn't.

Fran But you don't. Tell the truth. It would be so much easier.

Nick It's just . . .

Fran Yes?

Nick You'd be determined to have a bad time.

Fran Thanks. Thanks a lot.

Nick Wouldn't you?

Fran Thank you very much, Nick.

Nick Oh, fine. Is that it? Are you satisfied? Are we at the bottom now? You keep fucking asking . . . you keep asking . . . jabbing away . . . and then I tell you and you get all . . . Jesus. You asked, Fran.

Fran Maybe I've got it all wrong. Maybe there is no process to tell me about. Maybe I'm so far away it takes two hours to get round to a thing like this nowadays.

Nick Fran, look at me. I want you to come.

Fran The words well-spaced, the sentence complete.

Nick Well?

Fran I remember when your eyes . . .

Nick No. Stop. I want you to come. End of story. Stop all this. I just want you to come . . . all right? You need a break. Sleep and eat . . . all that.

Fran All right, Nick.

Nick All right. We can watch Martin and Darling do their thing.

Fran Yes.

Nick The death of hope. Cynicism, greed, opportunism, lust . . . all in a kind of sick contract.

Fran Have we finished?

Nick What?

Fran Our talk.

Nick It's like they have an agreement. Eyes open; tits out; willy and wonga; dosh and donga. Terrifying really.

Fran We're lucky.

Nick Terrifying.

Fran Aren't we, Nick?

Nick Yeah.

Fran I'm sorry. I'm sorry, Nick.

Nick It's all right.

Fran It's just . . . I miss you.

Nick Then you better come to Sussex.

Fran Will you promise me something?

Nick Anything.

Fran Something. Talk to me as much as you talk to them.

Nick God, Fran.

Fran You know what I mean. Don't go off. Don't get on a different bus.

Nick A different bus?

Fran A different bus. Did I say that?

Nick You said that.

Fran That's the stupidest . . .

Nick It's the stupidest thing you've ever said, doctor.

Fran Sorry.

Nick   That's all right.

Fran   I love you.

Nick   'Baby I Love You'. The Ronettes or The Ramones?

Fran   It's not that easy, Nick.

Nick   No.

Fran   Charm isn't enough.

Nick   No.

Fran   The Ronettes.

Nick   Why?

Fran   They took themselves seriously. The Ramones were self-conscious. They knew how they looked. Camp isn't camp when it calls itself camp.

Nick   You're right. You're always right.

Fran   Cuddle.

Nick   Cuddle.

They cuddle.

I've got a bit of work to do.

Fran   It's late.

Nick   Is it?

Fran   Yes. I'll be asleep.

Nick   OK.

Fran   Night.

Nick   Night.

Fran   Nick . . .

Nick   I love you too.

Fran   Nabokov collected butterflies.

Nick   Did he?

Fran   Yes.

Nick   I should . . .

Fran   Work.

Nick   Yes.

Fran   Not a complete hag.

Nick   No.

Fran   Poor Mary Duggan.

Nick   Yeah.

Scenes from an Execution by Howard Barker

Galactia, forties; Carpeta, thirties; any accent.

Venice, 1570s. Galactia is an esteemed painter and is currently under commission by the state to paint an enormous canvas celebrating the recent slaughtering of the infidel – Cypriots and Turks – at the Battle of Lepanto, a victory for Venetian Christians. When she mentions the dead men floating with their arses in the air, she is referring literally to the research she has been conducting for her realistic appraisal of this battle. She is expected to create a homage to the glory of the Venetians but she has something much more realistic in mind: a bloodbath. She sees it as her duty to speak for the dead, although she knows this will land her in prison, as it indeed does at the end of the play. Here, in the opening scene, Galactia is painting her long-term lover, Carpeta. He is also a painter, but currently not successful, other than for his mass-produced depiction of Christ with the flock. Nevertheless, he does love this impossibly difficult, intelligent and enquiring woman, who exasperates him in equal measure.

Galactia   Dead men float with their arses in the air. Hating the living, they turn their buttocks up. I have this on authority. Their faces meanwhile peer into the seabed where their bones will lie. After the battle the waves were clotted with men's bums, reproachful bums bobbing the breakers, shoals of matted buttocks, silent pathos in little bays at dawn. The thing we sit on has a character. Yours says to me KINDNESS WITHOUT INTEGRITY. I don't think you will ever leave your wife.

Carpeta   I shall leave my wife, I have every intention of leaving my –

Galactia No, you never will. I believed you would until I started this drawing, and now I see, your bum is eloquent on the subject, it is a bum that does not care to move . . .

Carpeta I resent that, Galactia –

Galactia You resent it –

Carpeta I resent it and I –

Galactia Resentment is such a miserable emotion. In fact it's not an emotion at all, it's a little twitch of self-esteem. Why resent when you can hate? DON'T MOVE!

Carpeta You are the most unsympathetic, selfish woman I have ever had the misfortune to become entangled with. You are arrogant and vain and you are not even very good-looking, in fact the contrary is the case and yet –

Galactia You are moving –

Carpeta I couldn't care if I am moving, I have my –

Galactia You are spoiling the drawing –

Carpeta I have my pride as well as you, and I will not lie here and be attacked like this, you have robbed me of all my resources, I am exhausted by you and my work is going to the –

Galactia What work?

Carpeta I HAVE DONE NO WORK!

Galactia Carpeta, you know perfectly well you only stand to benefit from the loss of concentration you have suffered through loving me. You have painted Christ among the flocks eight times now, you must allow the public some relief –

Carpeta YOU DESPISE ME!

Galactia Yes, I think I do. But kiss me, you have such a wonderful mouth.

Carpeta I won't kiss you.

Galactia Please, I have a passion for your lips.

Carpeta No, I will not. How can you love someone you despise?

Galactia I don't know, it's peculiar.

Carpeta Where are my trousers?

Galactia I adore you, Carpeta . . .

Carpeta I AM A BETTER PAINTER THAN YOU.

Galactia Yes –

Carpeta FACT.

Galactia I said yes, didn't I?

Carpeta And I have painted Christ among the flocks eight times not because I cannot think of anything else to paint but because I have a passion for perfection, I long to be the finest Christ painter in Italy, I have a longing for it, and that is something an opportunist like you could never understand –

Galactia No –

Carpeta You are ambitious and ruthless –

Galactia Yes –

Carpeta And you will never make a decent job of anything because you are a sensualist, you are a woman and a sensualist and you only get these staggering commissions from the state because you –

Galactia What?

Carpeta You –

Galactia   What?

Carpeta   Thrust yourself!

Galactia   I what?

Carpeta   Oh, let's not insult each other.

Galactia   Thrust myself?

Carpeta   Descend to low abuse –

Galactia   IT'S YOU WHO –

Carpeta   I am tired and I refuse to argue with you –

Galactia   Get out of my studio, then, go on, get out –

Carpeta   Here we go, the old Galactia –

Galactia   You are such a hypocrite, such an exhausting, dispiriting hypocrite, just get out –

Carpeta   As soon as I've got my trousers –

Galactia   NO, JUST GET OUT.

Serving it Up by David Eldridge

Sonny and Wendy, both twenty-one, both London accents.

Set in east London, Sonny and Wendy have known each other for years. Sonny doesn't work, he draws benefits and does some small-time drug dealing (the play's title is London slang for this); work is for mugs. Recently, Sonny has decided it is time to make a move on Wendy. They had a double date with Wendy's best friend Teresa and his best friend Nick, which didn't go well. Added to which, Sonny's father happened to be in the pub, on typical top form, deeply embarrassing his son. As Sonny appears, Teresa and Wendy have just had argument; Teresa has been moody and dissatisfied with everything lately, and Wendy is fed up with it all. These young people live in a world of casual violence, where verbal swagger and rage come easily.

Sonny *wanders over to the park bench and sits down. Pause.*

Sonny Cheers for coming, Wend.

Wendy Don't call me Wend. My name's Wendy.

Sonny Wendy – I'm sorry.

Wendy What do you want?

Sonny The pub – I'm sorry. The bloke who turned up.

Wendy Who, your uncle.

Sonny Yeah. Well, no. He's not my uncle. He's my dad.

Wendy So?

Sonny   Well, I know he embarrassed you and Trese.

Wendy   Oh yeah?

Sonny   We were all right till he turned up.

Wendy   Was that it?

Sonny   What, Wend? I'm trying to say sorry.

Wendy   I don't care if he's your dad.

Sonny   I brought you some flowers.

Pause.

Wendy   Who told you to do that?

Sonny   I thought of them.

Wendy   Great imagination.

Sonny   Don't take the piss. I thought you would like them.

Wendy   Like I said, great imagination.

Sonny   Why did you come here if you just want to take the piss?

Wendy   Because I'm as fucking sad as you are.

Pause.

Sonny   You met me at the pub.

Wendy   My whole life revolves around washing hair for one-fifty an hour. For a minute the thought of going out for a drink sounded exciting.

Pause.

Sonny   You went Bognor, didn't you?

Wendy   Fucking shit that was. Pissed down all day Saturday and all day Sunday and Teresa didn't stop moaning.

Sonny   I don't know why you hang about with her, Wend . . .

Wendy   Silly bitch thinks she's pregnant.

Sonny   Teresa? I thought she was right frigid.

Wendy   Yeah – well . . . She just pisses me off sometimes, that's all . . .

Pause.

Sonny   Me Aunt Viv had her baby yesterday. They're calling it Alexandria.

Wendy   Alexandria?

Sonny   Shit, innit?

Pause.

I reckon that – that you would feel better about things if you had someone.

Wendy   What?

Sonny   A bloke, like.

Wendy *laughs.*

Sonny   I can't say this very good. But – I think you're – beautiful.

Wendy   Shit. You just don't give up.

Sonny   I well fancy you, Wend . . .

Wendy *laughs.*

Sonny   Don't fucking laugh at me! I mean it!

Pause.

Wendy   You're unreal.

Sonny   I mean it, Wend. I've always liked you.

Wendy No, Sonny.

Sonny Come on, Wend, give us a go.

Wendy I'm not a piece of meat, Sonny.

Sonny I really mean it, Wendy.

Pause.

I've got some dough on me now. We could go up west, go to the pictures in Leicester Square, it'll be great.

Wendy If I wanted to be bought I'd be knocking about down Commerical Road.

Sonny I would pay anything in the world to have you.

Pause. **Sonny** *takes out a packet of cigarettes, gives one to* **Wendy**, *puts one in his own mouth and then takes out a box of matches. He shakes it. No sound – it's empty.*

You got a match, Wend?

Wendy My arse, your face.

Sonny *grins and* **Wendy** *lights the cigarette with her Zippo.*

Sonny Look at the kids over there, Wend. I used to be like that. Used to stand on top of the slide, look all around me at London. All them flats.

Pause. **Sonny** *pulls out his hanky and blows his nose making a disgusting noise.*

Wendy Sonny, that's disgusting. You're just like my brother.

Sonny Jimmy? Thought you'd disowned him.

Wendy No.

Sonny He's a fucking disgrace.

Wendy   You've got a cheek. He's not gay. He's just confused.

Sonny   That's what they all say. Just you keep him away from the school gates . . .

Wendy   Piss off!

Stitching by Anthony Neilson

Abby and Stu, both thirty, any accent.

This is a disturbing story of a couple who love each other but for whom love is not enough. It investigates the seamier side of sexual fantasy and role play within a couple's attempt to connect after four years together. The scenes in the play aren't sequential; they move back and forth in time, and it is never quite clear which is the present, or indeed what is reality and what is role play. The 'Stitching' of the title is particularly eloquent in this scene, as a faithless couple pick apart their relationship – stitch by painful stitch – while toasting the news that Abby is pregnant.

Stu (*off*)   Where's the corkscrew?

Abby   Isn't it in the drawer?

Stu (*off*)   No, obviously not. . .

Abby   It was there this morning . . .

Pause. **Stu** *enters, carrying a bottle of wine, two glasses and the corkscrew. He gets on with uncorking the wine.*

Abby   Where was it?

He pretends not to hear.

Stu   What?

Abby   The corkscrew.

Stu (*grumbling*)   Right at the fucking back . . .

Abby Right at the fucking back of the drawer?

He ignores her baiting. He hands her a glass of wine.

Stu Well?

Abby Well what?

Stu I don't know. Congratulations, I guess.

Abby Congratulations.

Stu Well, it means we're fertile, doesn't it?

Abby I never doubted that we were.

Stu I did.

Abby I know. That's why I'm pregnant.

Pause. She touches her glass to his.

To fertility.

They drink. Pause.

Of course I never meant to fall for you.

Stu So you keep saying.

Abby You know what did it?

Stu My stunning physique?

Abby No, it was a dream I had.

Stu A dream?

Abby Did I never tell you this?

Pause.

Stu Don't think so.

Abby It's stupid, really. I had a dream we were living with each other. And in the dream, we loved each other; and it felt all right, it felt good. And then, when I woke up – all of a sudden, I did.

Stu Did what?

Abby Loved you. (*Pause.*) All right, not loved you, not right away, but I felt close to you; and suddenly it was a possibility that I could.

Pause.

Is that bad?

Stu What, that our entire relationship is based on a dream?

Abby Not based on it. If you'd turned out to be a total cunt, I wouldn't have stuck with it because of the dream.

Stu I thought I did turn out to be a total cunt.

Abby Did you?

Stu I don't know. That's just what I took from you calling me a total cunt.

Abby When did I call you a total cunt?

Stu What day is it?

Abby Tuesday.

Stu Monday.

Abby Yes, well, on Monday, you were a total cunt.

Pause.

Stu So if you hadn't had this dream . . . ?

Abby Oh I wish I hadn't told you now!

Stu I'm glad you did.

Abby It's not a big deal.

Stu No: just a bit disturbing to find out our whole relationship's based on a dream.

She sighs. Pause.

Abby Anyway, they're all based on a dream. The house, the kids, the dog; the happily-ever-after. That's what hurts when you lose them. That's what you lose; the little dream you had.

Stu You lose the person.

Abby No you don't.

Stu It's losing the person that hurts, not some dream.

Abby No, because you don't lose the person. If we split up, you won't lose *me*. I'll still be around. What you'd lose is – our possible future.

Pause.

Stu Is that what we're talking about here? That if we don't have this child, it's over?

Abby What would be the point in going on?

Stu See, it's you that'd lose a dream or a future, not me. Cos I don't think this is about whether we have a kid, *full stop*. This is just about whether we have a kid right now.

Abby No it isn't. You know it isn't.

Stu Do I?

Abby Yes because I don't have the *time* to fuck around, Stuart –

Stu Didn't stop you before.

Pause.

Abby Do you want to go down that road? Do you? Do you really want to go down that road?

Stu No –

Abby Because I can go down that road if you want.

Stu No, I don't, I'm sorry. I don't want to go down that road. I'm sorry. I understand what you're saying about not having time but I just think you're exaggerating.

Abby Don't tell me I'm exaggerating! I know how I feel.

Stu You're only thirty . . .

Abby Yes and so I hang around for *another* four years waiting for you, do I? What happens then? Then I have to find someone else and then when I've found them, I have to figure out whether I want to have kids with them and then bang, I'm forty!

Stu Oooh, *forty*!

Abby Well maybe I want to have more than one kid. And it takes a lot of energy to bring up children – it's *tiring* – !

Stu You're assuming in four years I'd say no but maybe I wouldn't; we'd be a bit more settled, have our careers sorted out –

Abby No, fuck off, no: we don't have this child, that's it for us.

The enormity of what she's said hangs in the air, shocking even her.

I would hold it against you. I know I would.

Stu That's blackmail.

Abby Call it what you want but that's it, it has to be. For me, it does, and that's just it.

Pause. She leaves. He pours himself another drink.

Sweetheart by Nick Grosso

Charlie and Ruby, both early to mid twenties, London accents.

Charlie is out to have a good time, as usual, and who should he run into when he's clubbing, but Ruby, one-time girlfriend of his mate Tone. Once part of the same north London social scene, they've not seen each other for ages, not since she and Tone split up, in fact. The mutual attraction they could never admit to is still there, even if each is a bit shy about letting the other know.

This extract, which is the opening scene of the play, is as much about the language and the style of their particular communication as it is about what they're saying and, indeed, what they're not saying.

Charlie   hi ruby

Ruby   oh hiya!

Charlie   hi

Ruby   hi

Charlie   how's it going?

Ruby   okay

Charlie   i haven't seen you in years

Ruby   i know

Charlie   how's it going?

Ruby   okay

Pause.

Charlie how's it going?

Ruby okay

Charlie it's funny you know

Ruby what is?

Charlie i'm telling ya

Ruby what?

Charlie i was talking about you today

Ruby were you?

Charlie yeah

Ruby really?

Charlie yeah

Ruby with who?

Charlie i saw rachel on the tube

Ruby did you? how is she?

Charlie she's okay, i was sitting opposite her for ages then i thought 'shit that's wotserface innit' – i couldn't remember her name

Ruby rachel

Charlie yeah, i know, i thought about it for two stops and then i remembered

Charlie *and* **Ruby** rachel

Charlie yeah, so i leans forward and she thinks i'm about to rape her

Ruby *laughs.*

Charlie   you know what she's like, she's about to swipe me with her *big issue* dya know what i mean?

Ruby   didn't she recognize you?

Charlie   no

Ruby   that's surprising

Charlie   i know, so i go 'excuse me . . .'

[**Ruby**'s *friends confer.*]

'aren't you rachel?'

[**Friend I**   ruby we're going inside]

Ruby   okay

Ruby's *friends walk off.*]

Charlie   shit i'm not butting in am i?

Ruby   no

Charlie   we weren't rude?

Ruby   they'll never talk to me again

Charlie   stroppy cows

They laugh.

are they your friends?

Ruby   yeah

Charlie   i didn't mean . . . i'm sure they're . . . nice people

Ruby   they are

Charlie   they could learn some manners

Ruby   they're from broken homes

Charlie   it shows

They laugh.

so i goes . . .

Ruby   yeah

Charlie   'are you rachel?'

Ruby   yeah

Charlie   and she goes 'yeah' . . . she don't recognize me though

Ruby   that's surprising

Charlie   i know. so i goes *'it's charlie!'*

Ruby *laughs.*

Charlie   and she chills and we chat and that and she asks if i ever see you

Ruby   does she?

Charlie   yeah, so i say no – not since you split up with . . .
anyway . . .

Ruby *laughs coyly.*

Charlie   i explained it all to her don't worry

Ruby *laughs coyly.*

Charlie   so she says if i see you to say hello but i said there was fat chance of that but she said if i did so i said okay and then what dya know i see ya here on the *very same fucking day after all these years*!

He shakes his head in wonder.

unbelievable

Ruby   how is she?

Charlie   oh ya know

Ruby   what's she doing?

Charlie   she's a research assistant or something

Ruby   is she?

Charlie   for some TV firm . . . everyone's in TV these days have ya noticed?

Ruby   i know

Charlie   it's a scandal. what do you do?

Ruby   i'm a casting assistant

Charlie   what?

Ruby *laughs.*

Ruby   a casting assistant

Charlie   what's that?

Ruby   i assist casting

Charlie   do ya?

Ruby *nods.*

Charlie   what's that then?

Ruby   well you know how you might have a guinness commercial

Charlie   yeah

Ruby   and there's all those ordinary people on the street saying why they like guinness

Charlie   no i musta missed that one

Ruby   no i'm just saying . . . for instance

Charlie   oh yeah

They laugh.

Ruby   well *i* find those people

Pause.

Charlie   *you* find those people?

Ruby   yeah

Charlie   that's your job?

Ruby   yeah

Charlie   shit

Ruby   it's not that easy . . . you have to find the right people with the right faces and the right voices . . . and the right 'feel' about them . . . it's not that easy

Charlie   shit

Ruby *laughs.*

Charlie   so where dya find these people?

Ruby   we look them up on our files . . . or we phone around . . . and ask people . . . you know

Charlie   you mean actors?

Ruby   no

Charlie   what?

Ruby   real people

Charlie   what – you mean you use *real* people?

Ruby   yeah

Charlie   what – like me?

Ruby   yeah

Charlie   shit . . . i always thought they were actors

Two by Jim Cartwright

Roy and Lesley, any age between late teens and forty, with northern accents.

Two is a series of two-handers depicting working-class pub life, featuring the pub owner, his wife and their customers. All the parts are played by just two actors, so the whole play serves as an excellent radio exercise in versatility.

   In this section, demure Lesley is dominated by her jealous and controlling husband Roy. He's got an eye on what's happening around them, it's a busy night; she's just trying not to say the wrong thing.

Roy *comes over with drinks.*

Roy   What were he on about?

Lesley   Nowt, he were just collecting glasses.

Roy   Oh. Here you are. (*Puts drinks down. Sits.*) She's a character that landlady.

Lesley   She is.

They drink. Pause.

What you on?

Roy   Mild.

She nods. They sit in silence.

There's more strange things happen in a pub than there do on TV. Eh?

Lesley   Aye. Could I just . . . ?

Roy   Bloody hell, what did your last slave die of? Bloody hell! I've only just sat down.

Lesley   No. I wanted to know if I could go to loo.

Roy   'Course you can. Okay go.

She stands up.

But don't be long.

She begins to move.

Hey, and look down.

Lesley   Eh?

Roy   Keep your eyes down. Every time you look up, you look at men you.

Lesley   I don't.

Roy (*pointing at her*)   Eh, hey, no back chat. (*Looks quickly around, making sure no one's heard him.*) Go on.

She goes.

Roy (*to someone*)   Mike.

Pause.

(*To someone else.*) Sandy.

Pause.

She comes back and sits.

Roy   What did you have?

Lesley   Eh?

Roy   What did you have, one or two?

Lesley   One.

Roy You were a long time for a one.

Lesley There was someone in as well.

Roy Christ, I s'pose you got chatting.

Lesley No.

Roy No.

Lesley No.

Roy Don't 'no' me.

She edges back.

Did you say 'owt about me?

Lesley No.

Roy Who did you talk about then, someone else?

Lesley No.

Roy I told you with your no's. Who did you talk about?

Lesley We didn't even talk.

Roy Didn't even talk. Don't gi' me that. Two women in a woman's shithouse and they don't speak. You must think I'm soft. Do you?

Lesley What?

Roy Think I'm soft.

Lesley I don't know.

Roy What do you mean, don't know?

Lesley Well, I can't say no you said.

Roy Oh, if I said put your hand in the fire would you? Would you?

She shakes her head.

Why not?

She looks away.

No but you can talk about men in women's toilets can't you love, eh?

She keeps looking away.

If you don't answer, that means yes.

Lesley No.

Roy If you say no, two things happen: one I know you're lying, two I think about hittin' you in the face.

Lesley *looks down. He nods to someone across bar.*

Roy So, do you wanna stay here or move on?

Lesley Mmm.

Roy Christ I don't know why I bother. You've no conversation have you? Have you?

Lesley Mmm.

Roy See what I'm on about. I might as well go out with a piece of shit from that favourite woman's bog of yours, where you spent all our night.

Pause.

Do you want some more crisps?

Lesley Mmm.

Roy Well liven up then and you might get some later on. What about some 'Wotsits'?

Lesley Yes.

Roy Well there you are then. Liven up and you might get some 'Wotsits'.

Pause.

They've done a nice job in here 'ant they, eh? He did a lot of it himself, knocked the snug out and everything. What's over there?

Lesley Eh?

Roy What's over there so interesting?

Lesley Nothing, I just moved me head I . . .

Roy I see. Watching the darts were you? Eh?

Lesley No I . . .

Roy What?

Lesley I don't know.

Roy Don't know. I do. See that little git in the jeans and shirt, there, him.

She looks.

Okay you've seen enough now. Well I could break him like that, with my knee and my arms. Break the little wanker like that. Okay? Okay?

Lesley Okay.

Roy Would you be sad?

Lesley I don't know. I don't even know him.

Roy But you'd like to wouldn't you?

Lesley No.

Roy No. Are you sure?

She nods her head.

It's just that 'okay' sounded a bit sad.

Lesley   What 'okay'?

Roy   That 'okay' you said before sounded a bit sad. After I'd said I'd break the little wanker. That one.

Lesley (*confused*)   Oh.

Roy *stares at her a long time.*

Roy   Don't make me feel small.

Lesley   I'm not.

Roy   I'm not having you or him or anyone making me feel small.

Lesley   I'm not.

Roy   Well, I just said all that then, and then felt small.

Lesley   What?

Roy   About him and you, and that 'okay', and you made me feel small after. When it was your fault, I said it in the first place, for looking at him.

Lesley (*beaten*)   Oh.

Roy   Well.

Lesley   What?

Roy   Are you not going to say sorry?

Lesley   Sorry.

Roy   Right. (*To someone across bar, raises his glass.*) Aye get 'em down yeah. Ha.

Silence.

You've gone quiet. What you thinking of?

Lesley   Nothing.

Roy No, no. Hold on. No. Who you thinking of?

Lesley (*pleading*) Oh Roy.

Roy No, no. When someone's quiet they're thinking, right?

Lesley Maybe.

Roy Maybe. That's a funny word to say, maybe. What you saying maybe for? That means you were. Who?

Lesley I wasn't.

Roy Who? If you wasn't, you would have said no. Who were you thinking of?

Lesley No one.

Roy Who? (*Waits.*) Who?

She shakes her head.

Hey, remember what I said about no. Who?

She looks down.

Who?

She looks down more.

Who?

Lesley (*suddenly jumps up*) No one. No one at all. Can't I even have me own mind!

Roy (*embarrassed*) Sit down. Sit down.

Lesley I can't win. If I said I was thinking of every man in here naked, or I said I was thinking of you and the baby, it wouldn't make any difference. You'd still find a way of torturing me wouldn't you? Torturing! Torturing!

She storms out.

He looks round grinning, embarrassed.

Pause.

She comes back in.

Lesley   I need the front door key.

Roy (*gently*)   Hey, sit down love. Please sit.

She still stands.

I'm sorry. I realise what I must have done to you now. I don't know what it is. It's 'cause I care like. You know. I get carried away. Come on, sit down, please.

She does.

(*Soft.*) I didn't expect you to do that love.

Suddenly slaps her.

(*Vicious.*) You'll never do it again.

Vongole by Michael Butt

Tristram, forty plus, RP or any appropriate accent; Helen, early twenties, any accent.

Seriously attractive Oxford don Tristram Swann is an authority on the works of the Italian Renaissance poet Petrarch. Still reeling from the break-up of his marriage to the ideal Judy, he pursues nubile research assistants like Helen, taking them to romantic Italian locations in the hope of rekindling the passion of his times there with his wife. Unfortunately, their more carnal desires only serve to disappoint him in his quest for perfect love, his special interest. Perfection can be bewilderingly unattainable, but Tristram doesn't let that stop him looking for it relentlessly. The memory of one distant idyllic night with Judy drives him on, and centres on the consumption of *vongole* (clams). He's trying to recapture that exact moment of bliss, but it's elusive. Helen, meanwhile, is after something much more basic.

These excerpts come from an early part of the play: they can stand alone but together offer very different acting challenges. It begins in Tristram's rooms at the university.

Tristram   Tell me, could you imagine that northern Italy in late spring might provide a convenient jumping-off place for a rewarding friendship?

Helen   I could.

Tristram   Would you take the plunge in Venice?

Helen   I would.

Tristram   Excellent. May I ask you a question?

Helen   Be my guest.

Tristram   Do you like pasta?

A hotel in Venice.

Tristram *and* **Helen** *in bed.*

Helen   Oh . . . I love Venice!

Tristram   Yes. Don't you think it's time we got up?

Helen   Why?

Tristram   Well . . . there's a city out there.

Helen   Is it as nice as this?

Pause.

Tristram   It's different.

Helen   I'm not interested.

Tristram   It's a very interesting city, Venice.

Helen   Mmm.

Tristram   There's, em . . . the . . . Palace of the Doges . . .

Helen   Oh yeh?

She starts stroking him.

Tristram   That's eh . . . oh, oh . . . St Mark's . . . Ah, Helen!

Helen   St Mark's? Wow. What's that, some kind of church?

Tristram   Oh! Oh!

Helen   Is that a yes?

Tristram   Yes!

Helen   I'm not hurting you, am I?

Tristram   Ahhhh!

Helen   We'll go later, shall we?

Tristram   The thing is . . .

Helen   What?

Tristram   . . . the thing . . . Helen . . . is . . .

Helen   What?

Tristram   . . . I'm hungry.

Helen   We ate two hours ago.

Tristram   Yes. I saw a little restaurant . . .

Helen   Did you?

Tristram   . . . from the gondola.

Helen   I see.

Tristram   Looked very enchanting and . . . all lit up, little lights . . . and I said to myself: 'Helen would love that, must take Helen there.'

Helen   Right.

Tristram   Having a nice time, aren't we, Helen?

Pause.

Helen   Oh yes.

She grabs him hard.

Tristram   Ah!

A restaurant in Venice.

They are looking at a menu.

Helen   *Zuppa di cozze?*

Tristram   No. I don't think so.

Pause.

Helen   How about the *tagliatelle con i funghi*?

Tristram (*negative*)   Nnn nn

Pause.

Helen   So what would you say to the *spaghetti alla puttanesca*?

Tristram   I don't think so, Helen.

Pause.

Helen   OK, you've dragged me here –

Tristram   Dragged?

Helen   Sorry?

Tristram   I don't . . . I don't . . . I don't recall dragging you, that's all.

Pause.

Helen   You conveyed me here . . .

Tristram   On a very nice water boat.

Helen   The vehicle is neither here nor there . . . Tristram . . .

Tristram   Right.

Helen   It doesn't matter. What do you want to eat?

Pause.

Tristram   Do you know . . . ?

Helen   Yes?

Tristram   Do you know . . . I think I'll go for the *vongole*.

What If It's Raining? by Anthony Minghella

Dominic and Marilyn, both early thirties, both any accent.

Dominic's wife Marilyn has been having an affair with his friend Philip for some time, partly in reaction to Dominic's constant preoccupation with work and lack of emotional commitment, and partly her frustration with feeling that she runs the house and brings up baby Jack by herself. Neither has made an art of truthfully expressing their feelings to one another and it's reached a point of no return. She has finally told him that she is leaving to set up home with Philip in distant Bristol, and here she is unhappily sorting through the possessions accumulated during their marriage in readiness for her and Jack's imminent departure.

Dominic is crushed by the unexpected change of circumstances and finds himself in a sequence of events that he can't control. Not certain that she's doing the right thing but determined to go, Marilyn also feels overwhelmed by how easily and utterly her seemingly perfect and stable family life has fallen apart.

Marilyn *is on her knees in the sitting room, sorting out books and records into two piles, hers and* **Dominic***'s.* **Dominic** *returns, having put* **Jack** *to bed.*

Dominic   He was really exhausted. He almost dropped off when I was drying him after the bath. (*He kneels down by the books.*) Which pile's yours?

Marilyn   This one.

Dominic *takes a book from 'his' pile.*

Dominic   Oh. Is this mine?

Marilyn   Well . . . it was a Christmas present to us both from your aunt in Greenwich. I think that means you keep it.

Dominic   I've never looked at it. Do you want it?

Marilyn   No.

Dominic (*as they continue sorting*)   What's happening about the move?

Marilyn   Philip's coming with a van in the morning.

Dominic   Tomorrow?

Pause.

Marilyn   Yeah.

Dominic   A van full, huh?

Marilyn   There's all Jack's things. His cot, and stuff. And the highchair.

Dominic   Right.

They continue.

Marilyn   You don't have to do this, Dom. I can manage.

Dominic   It's okay. What else are you taking besides your books?

Marilyn   Oh, maybe my records. Some clothes.

Dominic   What about furniture?

Marilyn   Well, I don't know. What do you think?

Dominic (*meaning it*)   Take whatever you want.

Marilyn   Actually, the thing which I'd . . . I could really do with, but I mean, obviously if . . .

Dominic   What?

Marilyn   The bed.

Dominic (*this registers*)   Right.

Marilyn   It's just that I mean you know it's what I need for my back and the one Philip has is no good and . . .

Dominic   No, take it. (*Pause.*) I probably wouldn't be able to sleep in it again anyway.

Marilyn   It's a bed, Dominic.

Dominic   Yeah.

Marilyn   But thanks. That's kind.

Dominic   Listen, Marilyn. I don't care. It's not kindness. You're going. Jack's going. The possessions – the things in this place – are neither here nor there. If I come back tomorrow and the house is empty, it really wouldn't bother me.

Marilyn   Well obviously, there's no question –

Dominic   Oh, I'd like to keep the stereo.

Marilyn (*she wanted it*)   Okay.

Dominic   Unless you particularly . . .

Marilyn   No it's fine. Could I have the radio-cassette then?

Dominic   Fine.

Marilyn   And I would be grateful if I could have the washing machine.

Dominic (*surprised*)   Philip doesn't have one?

Marilyn   No. And there's all the baby's stuff . . . nappies and, well, you know, there's half a house to wash every day. I really couldn't manage without –

Dominic   No, no. I said . . . whatever you want.

Marilyn   I'd rather you knew what I was taking. And agree.

Dominic   What about the car?

Marilyn   I don't know.

Marilyn *wants the car. So does* **Dominic**. *He's also begun to contemplate all the other things he'd like to keep.*

Dominic   Well, the thing is, if you take the car, how do I get to see Jack? (*A pause.*) That is allowed?

Marilyn   Don't be stupid. You know you can see him as much as you like.

Dominic   Every day? (*No response.*) Anyway, that's the problem as regards the car.

Pause.

Marilyn   It's very easy by train.

Dominic   Yeah, but when I get to the other end, then what?

Marilyn   In what sense?

Dominic   Well, do I have to say yes or no this minute?

Marilyn   Well obviously not.

There's a sheet of paper on the floor. **Dominic** *picks it up, examines it.*

Dominic   Is this the list of things you wanted to take with you?

Marilyn   I mean, I hadn't actually intended for you to read it. It's just to jog my thoughts.

Dominic (*looking down the list*)   Doesn't Philip have cutlery?

Marilyn   I don't know. I don't want to be dependent on him. I'd rather have things which . . . Anyway, we got two sets from our wedding presents. You don't need them both.

Dominic   No. I guess not. It's just that there are things here which I won't have but I'm sure Philip already has. The liquidiser . . . uh – the radio alarm – surely you don't want that? So you end up with two of something and . . .

Marilyn   He doesn't actually have a liquidiser, but anyway.

Dominic (*putting down the list*)   Look, this is silly. If I read this list I'll get . . . I'm getting frazzled here. I mean it when I say I'd prefer you just took the stuff . . . I probably won't even notice it's gone. Actually, I'll tell you what you *can* take.

Marilyn   What's that?

Dominic   The lawn mower.

Marilyn   Why?

Dominic   Haven't you got a garden in Bristol?

Marilyn   Hardly.

Dominic   Well, it'll come in handy.

Marilyn   What about the lawn? I bought you that lawn mower.

Dominic   I'll pay a Boy Scout to cut it once a year.

Marilyn   He'll still have to have something to cut it with.

Dominic   I don't care. He can use his teeth.

Pause.

Marilyn   Why didn't you say?

Dominic   That I hate gardening?

Marilyn   Yes.

Acknowledgements

p. 106   Extract from *Bedroom Farce* by Alan Ayckbourn. Copyright © 1975, 1977 Alan Ayckbourn. Reproduced by permission of Random House Ltd and Grove/Atlantic Inc. Performance rights enquiries: Casarotto Ramsay & Associates Ltd (www.casarotto.uk.com) / Samuel French Ltd (www.samuelfrench-london.co.uk) [amateur]

p. 137   Extract from *The Employee* by Sebastian Baczkiewicz. Copyright © 2005, Sebastian Baczkiewicz. Reproduced by permission of The Agency (London) Ltd and BBC Radio 4 (originally commissioned and broadcast by BBC Radio 4). Performance rights enquiries: The Agency (London) Ltd, 24 Pottery Lane, London W11 4LZ (info@theagency.co.uk)

p. 168   Extract from *Scenes from an Execution* by Howard Barker (Calder Publications Ltd). Copyright © 1985 Howard Barker. Reproduced by permission of Calder Publications Ltd. Performance rights enquiries: Judy Daish Associates Ltd, 2 St Charles Place, London W10 6EG

p. 150   Extract from *How Guillaume Apollinaire Saved my Marriage* by Michael Butt. Copyright © 2001 Michael Butt. Reproduced by permission of Mr M Butt. Performance rights enquiries: Mr M Butt (michaelbutt1@onetel.com)

p. 196   Extract from *Vongole* by Michael Butt. Copyright © 2003 Michael Butt. Reproduced by permission of Mr M Butt. Performance rights enquiries: Mr M Butt (michaelbutt1@onetel.com)

p. 158   Extract from *The Mortal Ash* by Richard Cameron from *Richard Cameron Plays: 1* (Methuen Publishing Ltd). Reproduced by

permission of Methuen. Copyright © 1994 Richard Cameron.
Performance rights enquiries: Curtis Brown Group Ltd
(cb@curtisbrown.co.uk)

p. 188   Extract from *Two* by Jim Cartwright from *Jim Cartwright
Plays: 1* (Methuen Publishing Ltd). First published as *To* in 1991.
Copyright © 1991, 1994 Jim Cartwright. Reproduced by permission
of Methuen and Angela Jones Associates. Performance rights
enquiries: Angela Jones Associates, Dept C, Higher Healey House,
Higherhouse Lane, White Coppice, Chorley, Lancashire, PR6 9BT /
Samuel French Ltd (www.samuelfrench-london.co.uk) [amateur]

p. 118   Extract from *The Country* by Martin Crimp (Faber &
Faber Ltd). Copyright © 2000, 2005 Martin Crimp. Reproduced by
permission of Faber & Faber Ltd. Performance rights enquiries: Judy
Daish Associates Ltd, 2 St Charles Place, London W10 6EG

p. 86   Extract from *The National Theatre* by David Edgar from
Edgar Shorts by David Edgar (Nick Hern Books Ltd). Copyright ©
1989 David Edgar. Reproduced by permission of Nick Hern Books
Ltd (www.nickhernbooks.co.uk). Performance rights enquiries: Alan
Brodie Representation Ltd (www.alanbrodie.com) / Samuel French
Ltd (www.samuelfrench-london.co.uk) [amateur]

p. 172   Extract from *Serving it Up* by David Eldridge from *David
Eldridge Plays: 1* (Methuen Publishing Ltd). Copyright © 1996, 2005
David Eldridge. Reproduced by permission of Methuen. Performance
rights enquiries: ICM, 76 Oxford Street, London W1N 0AX

p. 132   Extract from *Duck* by Sheila Feehily (Nick Hern Books
Ltd). Copyright © 2003 Sheila Feehily. Reproduced by permission of
Nick Hern Books Ltd (www.nickhernbooks.co.uk). Performance
rights enquiries: Nick Hern Books Ltd
(info@nickhernbooks.demon.co.uk)

p. 112   Extract from *The Bridge at Cookham* by Sheila Goff (commissioned and broadcast on BBC Radio 4). Copyright © 2000 Sheila Goff. Reproduced by permission of Felix de Wolfe. Performance rights enquiries: Felix de Wolfe, Kingsway House, 103 Kingsway, London WC2B 6QX

p. 142   Extract from and *File it Under Fiction* by Sheila Goff (commissioned for BBC Radio Drama). Copyright © 2002 Sheila Goff. Reproduced by permission of Felix de Wolfe. Performance rights enquiries: Felix de Wolfe, Kingsway House, 103 Kingsway, London WC2B 6QX

p. 182   Extract from *Sweetheart* by Nick Grosso (Faber & Faber Ltd). Copyright © 1996 Nick Grosso. Reproduced by permission of Faber & Faber Ltd. Performance rights enquiries: Casarotto Ramsay & Associates Ltd (www.casarotto.uk.com)

p. 67   Extract from *Inside Out* by Tanika Gupta (Oberon Books). Copyright © 2002 Tanika Gupta. Reproduced by permission of Oberon Books. Performance rights enquiries: The Agency (London) Ltd, 24 Pottery Lane, London W11 4LZ (info@theagency.co.uk)

pp. 21, 101 Extracts from *Beautiful Thing* by Jonathan Harvey from *Jonathan Harvey Plays: 1* (Methuen Publishing Ltd). Copyright © 1994 Jonathan Harvey. Reproduced by permission of Methuen. Performance rights enquiries: ICM, 76 Oxford Street, London W1N 0AX

p. 154   Extract from *Man with a Travel Hairdryer* by Katie Hims (originally commissioned and broadcast by BBC Radio 4). Copyright © 2005 Katie Hims. Reproduced by permission of Ms K Hims and BBC Radio 4. Performance rights enquiries: please contact Methuen in the first instance with details of your performance plans (all performance rights enquiries will be forwarded by Methuen to the author)

Acknowledgements

p. 124   Extract from *Dead Funny* by Terry Johnson (Methuen Publishing Ltd). Copyright © 1994 Terry Johnson. Reproduced by permission of Methuen and The Agency (London) Ltd. Performance rights enquiries: The Agency (London) Ltd, 24 Pottery Lane, London W11 4LZ (info@theagency.co.uk) / Samuel French Ltd (www.samuelfrench-london.co.uk) [amateur]. All rights reserved

p. 91   Extract from *Protection* by Fin Kennedy (Nick Hern Books Ltd). Copyright © 2003 Fin Kennedy. Reproduced by permission of Nick Hern Books Ltd (www.nickhernbooks.co.uk). Performance rights enquiries: Nick Hern Books Ltd (info@nickhernbooks.demon.co.uk) [amateur]

p. 200   Extract from *What If It's Raining?* by Anthony Minghella (Methuen Publishing Ltd). Copyright © 1989 Anthony Minghella. Reproduced by permission of Methuen. Performance rights enquiries: Judy Daish Associates Ltd, 2 St Charles Place, London W10 6EG

p. 162   Extract from *Nabokov's Gloves* by Peter Moffat from *Nabokov's Gloves and Iona Rain* (Methuen Publishing Ltd). Copyright © 1999 Peter Moffat. Reproduced by permission of PFD (www.pfd.co.uk) on behalf of Peter Moffat. Performance rights enquiries: PFD (www.pfd.co.uk) / Samuel French Ltd (www.samuelfrench-london.co.uk) [amateur]

p. 62   Extract from *Honour* by Joanna Murray-Smith (Nick Hern Books Ltd). Copyright © 1995, 1997, 2003 Joanna Murray-Smith. Reproduced by permission of Nick Hern Books Ltd, London, and Currency Press Pty Ltd, Sydney, Australia. Performance rights enquiries: Nick Hern Books Ltd (info@nickhernbooks.demon.co.uk) [amateur in the UK & Ireland only]

p. 177   Extract from *Stitching* by Anthony Neilson (Methuen Publishing Ltd). Coypright © 2002 Anthony Neilson. Reproduced by

permission of Methuen. Performance rights enquiries: Julia Tyrrell
Management Ltd, 57 Greenham Road, London N10 1LN
(julia@jtmanagement.co.uk)

p. 52   Extract from *Some Voices* by Joe Penhall from *Joe Penhall
Plays: 1* (Methuen Publishing Ltd). Copyright © 1995 Joe Penhall.
Reproduced by permission of Methuen. Performance rights
enquiries: Curtis Brown Group Ltd (cb@curtisbrown.co.uk)

p. 57   Extract from *Handbag* by Mark Ravenhill from *Mark
Ravenhill Plays: 1* (Methuen Publishing Ltd). Copyright © 1998 Mark
Ravenhill. Reproduced by permission of Methuen. Performance
rights enquiries: Casarotto Ramsay & Associates Ltd
(www.casarotto.uk.com)

p. 96   Extract from *Amadeus* by Peter Shaffer (Penguin).
Copyright © 1980, 1981 Peter Shaffer. Reproduced by permission of
Sir Peter Shaffer, The Lantz Office, New York & Penguin Books,
London. Performance rights enquiries: Macnaughton Lord 2000 Ltd,
19 Margravine Gardens, London W6 8RL (www.ml2000.org.uk);
Robert Lantz, The Lantz Office, 200 West 57th Street, New York, NY
10019, USA (tel: 001 212 586 0200 / fax: 001 212 262 6659 [US
performance rights]; Samuel French Ltd (www.samuelfrench-
london.co.uk) [amateur]

p. 46   Extract from *Other People* by Christopher Shinn
(Methuen Publishing Ltd). Copyright © 2000 Christopher Shinn.
Reproduced by permission of Methuen. Performance rights
enquiries: Dramatists Play Service, USA (www.dramatists.com)
[amateur]

p. 81   Extract from *The Memory of Water* by Shelagh
Stephenson from *Shelagh Stephenson Plays: 1* (Methuen Publishing
Ltd). Copyright © 1997 Shelagh Stephenson. Reproduced by
permission of Methuen. Performance rights enquiries: Julia Tyrrell

Acknowledgements

Management Ltd, 57 Greenham Road, London N10 1LN
(julia@jtmanagement.co.uk); Samuel French Ltd
(www.samuelfrench-london.co.uk) [amateur]

p. 15   Extract from *Art and Guff* by Catherine Tregenna
(Oberon Books). Copyright © 2001 Catherine Tregenna. Reproduced
by permission of Oberon Books. Performance rights enquiries: The
Agency (London) Ltd, 24 Pottery Lane, London W11 4LZ
(info@theagency.co.uk)

p. 34   Extract from *Burn the Aeneid!* by Martyn Wade.
Copyright © 1992 Martyn Wade. Reproduced by permission of Sheil
Land Associates Ltd on behalf of Martyn Wade. Performance rights
enquiries: Sheil Land Associates Ltd, 52 Doughty Street, London
WC1N 2LS (info@sheilland.co.uk)

p. 28   Extract from *Been So Long* by Che Walker (Faber & Faber
Ltd). Copyright © 1998 Che Walker. First published by Faber &
Faber Ltd. Reproduced by permission of The Agency (London) Ltd.
Performance rights enquiries: The Agency (London) Ltd, 24 Pottery
Lane, London W11 4LZ (info@theagency.co.uk). All rights reserved

p. 145   Extract from *Gulp* by Roger Williams from *New Welsh
Drama* (Parthian Books). Copyright © 1998 Roger Williams.
Reproduced by permission of Parthian Books, The Old Surgery,
Napier Street, Cardigan, SA43 1ED. Performance rights enquiries: Jill
Foster Ltd, 9 Barb Mews, Brook Green, London W6 7PA

p. 74   Extract from *Little Sweet Thing* by Roy Williams
(Methuen Publishing Ltd). Copyright © 2005 Roy Williams.
Reproduced by permission of Methuen. Performance rights
enquiries: Alan Brodie Representation Ltd (www.alanbrodie.com)

p. 40   Extract from *Dogs Barking* by Richard Zajdlic (Faber &
Faber Ltd). Copyright © 1999 Richard Zajdlic. Reproduced by

permission of Faber & Faber Ltd and PFD (www.pfd.co.uk) on behalf of Richard Zajdlic. Performance rights enquiries: PFD (www.pfd.co.uk)

Disclaimer

Methuen Drama gratefully acknowledges the
permissions granted to reproduce the quoted extracts within this
work. Every effort has been made to trace the current copyright
holders of the extracts included in this work. The publishers
apologise for any unintended omissions and would be pleased to
receive any information that would enable them to amend any
inaccuracies or omissions in future editions.

Caution Notice

All rights whatsoever in these plays are strictly reserved and
application for performance must be made *before* rehearsals
commence to the appropriate performance rights contact. No
performance may be given unless a licence has been obtained.